The Heart and
Other Monsters

The Heart and
Other Monsters

A Memoir

Rose Andersen

BLOOMSBURY PUBLISHING

NEW YORK · LONDON · OXFORD · NEW DELHI · SYDNEY

BLOOMSBURY PUBLISHING
Bloomsbury Publishing Inc.
1385 Broadway, New York, NY 10018, USA

BLOOMSBURY, BLOOMSBURY PUBLISHING, and the Diana logo
are trademarks of Bloomsbury Publishing Plc

First published in the United States, 2020

Although this memoir is primarily a work of nonfiction, the names,
locales, settings, and identifying characteristics of certain individuals have
been changed, and certain events have been disguised, to protect the
privacy of these individuals, and dialogue has been reconstructed to
the best of the author's recollection.

Photograph of Rick Springer on page 31 courtesy of Peter Drekmeier.
All other photos courtesy of the author.

ISBN: HB: 978-1-63557-514-9; eBook: 978-1-63557-515-6

LIBRARY OF CONGRESS CATALOGING-IN-PUBLICATION DATA IS AVAILABLE

2 4 6 8 10 9 7 5 3 1

Typeset by Westchester Publishing Services
Printed and bound in the U.S.A. by Berryville Graphics Inc.,
Berryville, Virginia

To find out more about our authors and books visit
www.bloomsbury.com and sign up for our newsletters.

Bloomsbury books may be purchased for business or promotional use.
For information on bulk purchases please contact Macmillan Corporate
and Premium Sales Department at specialmarkets@macmillan.com.

For the women that loved her

Carol
Sharon
Ilena
Tess

Had I known but yesterday what I know today,
I'd have taken out your two gray eyes
And put in eyes of clay;
And had I known but yesterday you'd be no more my own
I'd have taken out your heart of flesh
And put in one of stone

—TAM LIN

A NOTE TO THE READER

Throughout this book, I have speculated or imagined events concerning whether or not my sister was murdered. I have no outside knowledge or evidence not disclosed to readers about these speculations. The reader should not conclude that I have any concrete facts or proof that my sister was murdered.

PART I

The Girl

Her own sister, Janet, after years of failed suicide attempts, had killed herself by jumping off the Bay Bridge when Sharon was just twenty-eight years old. Their mother began showing signs of early-onset Alzheimer's within months of Janet's death. Sharon turned into her family's caretaker the second Janet stepped off the bridge and into the welcoming water. I put my hands on my stepmother's chest and told her she had to agree not to kill herself in response to Sarah's death. Two hours later, I would grab my mother's arm and make her promise the same thing.

One day my heart will stop thumping, and blood will stop circulating through my body. I will watch everyone's hearts run around this lovely, dim world; they glow from space. I will watch those bright, twinkling specks that stars gaze at. I will hear those hearts singing. They only know one refrain. It repeats through the universe as their valves open and close: love is not enough, love is not enough.

If only my heart were a time machine.

I would go back to that day on the couch with her.

I would say, if you die, it will ruin both our lives.

I will look for your body at every turn.

I will spend my life with your ghost running right behind me.

I will spend my days imagining the lives we could have had.

I will live in the ruins of your absence.

I will nightmare you alive in my sleep.

I will wake up and tell myself: don't let this death become what your days are made of, let it flicker on the horizon, give it a home only on the edges of your life. But some part of my brain will always be calling your name.

If you die, Sarah, the universe will never be the same.

The Girl

S he has spent the last few hours desperately texting the Man to come pick her up so they can go get some dope. It is early, just before sunrise, but she knows he will be awake. He picks her up in his beat-up Dodge truck. They drive to someone's house, and when heroin isn't available she settles for something else. A high is a high is a high. Her bones are beginning to chatter with withdrawal.

The Man drops her back off at her house, promising to swing by later, to take a few hits with her, after he runs an errand. Sarah promises to wait, but they both know she is lying.

After he leaves, she assembles the ribbon, the spoon, the ball of cotton, the needle, the cup of water, and sits on the floor of her bathroom, back against the door. She smokes a cigarette, enjoying the shooting pain in her legs for a moment because she knows it will be gone soon. The anticipation, at this point, is sometimes better than the hit.

She measures out some, then thinks, *What the fuck, a little more.* She puts the white powder on the spoon. It looks about right, the amount of H she typically does. She sets the spoon carefully on the tile floor, watches as it spends a millisecond finding its resting point before turning her attention to the syringe.

She puts the syringe into the cup and pulls up a little water. Carefully, she picks up the spoon and releases the water into it, using the tip of the needle to mix everything up. She likes this part, the dissolving of powder to milky wet wonder. Once that's done, she takes a small piece of cotton and rolls it between her fingers until it is the size and shape of a pea, a vegetable she hates. She puts the cotton ball into the spoon and lets it soak up what she has made.

She picks up her needle and gently places the tip into the cotton ball—which will filter out any larger chunks—and then slowly pulls the plunger back. The syringe is full and ready for her.

The needle is placed back on the floor while she ties herself off. She usually likes someone else to do this part and to inject her. The Man, Jack, Ryan. One of the many boys who love her. But she doesn't want to wait for the Man to come back; then she would have to share. She picks up the red ribbon and looks down at her thighs. She is skinny now, finally. But she is still worried the ribbon won't be long enough. It is, of course; she used it last night. Sometimes she wakes up and imagines all her fat has come back to her in her sleep.

She ties it tight. It takes a while to find a vein. She can't use her arms anymore; her veins have collapsed. But at the back of the knee, she still has one that lights up for her. It glows blue in the gray of early morning. She places the tip of the needle at the pulsing, shimmering center of the vein and slides it in. She is desperate, this close to the rush, but takes the time to pull the plunger back a little to make sure she has hit blood. For a second, the swirling red and white reminds her of cherry blossoms.

She pushes the plunger down, slow and steady, and her body relaxes instantly as the drug hits her system. Her brain begins to release dopamine rapidly, flooding her with something she would like to think is joy. Her body temperature rises, and she can feel her skin flush pink. She leans her head against the door and tries to enjoy the rush.

Her heart is beating hard, and she wishes she could place her hand inside her chest and hold it steady. She is positively vibrating. She can feel the heat travel from her throbbing knee toward her head. It doesn't feel like joy anymore, it feels like crackling flame. She can hear her dog pawing at the bathroom door, he doesn't like it when she is in here for a long time.

She tries to get up and open the door, but her hands and legs feel numb and like they are burning all at the same time. The dog begins to bark, but her ears are ringing and she wonders if he isn't just outside the door, maybe he is outside the house. He likes to run away, take off into the forest. When he does this, she takes a shirt she has recently worn and leaves it on the edge of the property so he can find his way back to her. He always does.

She tries to call out for him, tell him not to run, but her tongue feels heavy and swollen. Her skin is turning from pink to blue and the buzzing in her blood has almost reached her eyes. Once, when she was little, she jumped onto a log in the woods and broke open a wasp's nest. They enveloped her. She was a beautiful, humming monster until she was pulled away from the angry insects. Does she look like that now? Has her glowing vein lit up her whole body?

Her stomach clenches, and she wonders if she can throw up, wonders if her thick tongue will let the contents of her body leave. She tries to swallow but cannot feel her throat. The absence of throat makes her realize that she has never been aware of her esophagus before—it just existed. Until now, when she is sure it doesn't.

The hot, buzzing pressure has reached her head. She can feel her brain growing. *Don't do it*, she tells her brain. *There is not enough space for you to get any bigger.* Her brain does not listen. She can feel it pushing against her ears, trying to squeeze her eyeballs out of their sockets. *I need my eyes*, she thinks, but the pressure builds against her wishes.

She is suddenly scared. She is twenty-four. She doesn't like this. Heroin is much nicer, she prefers when she can hardly feel anything at all. Her vision blurs, and the early-morning light gives way to a blackness that seems to be saying her name. She can feel her limbs clench, trying to hold her inside her body. *Please*, she says. The drug releases a brilliant firework inside her head. *Oh*, she thinks, *so this—*

. . .

The Man stops by Sarah's house a little after eight. He knocks on the door, and when she doesn't answer, he begins to pound harder. He wants his share. He mutters "bitch" and leaves an angry note, written on a paper napkin he grabs from his car, on her door. This isn't the first time she has locked him out to get high on her own.

The dog barks. He growls. He claws at the door. He runs through the house, knocking over trash cans, upending the coffee table, pulling the cushions off the couch. He shits on the bed. He drinks from his water bowl until it is empty. He howls for four days.

A postman comes and delivers a package. He can hear a dog barking, but no one answers the door. He leaves the box on the front porch and leaves.

Jack returns home. He calls out for her. "What the fuck," he says, looking around the trashed house, seeing the hysterical dog. He walks to the bathroom door and pulls the door open. Before her body can hit the floor, he knows.

Spirit Gone

My mother and sister found a dead body once. We lived in a small town tucked between the bay and the ocean. They were walking through the dunes toward the beach. They came across a woman who had drowned and whose body returned to shore. She was beyond saving, white, cold, spirit gone. I have often wondered what she looked like: if they could see her eyes, whether her skin was turning gray. If I had been with my mother, I'd have clung to the memory of this day. My sister was no more than seven, and when she told me, she didn't seem rattled; she was more interested in reading the newest *Harry Potter*. Her friend Tess showed me a letter, only a few sentences long, that Sarah sent her.

> *Dear Tess, how are you? I am fine. You will never guess what happened to me a few days ago. Me and my mom were walking down the beach and we found a dead body.*

It was so scary. I know you think I am lying but I am not,
I am still really scared. I got the 4th Harry Potter book and
so far, it's really good, I bought two so you can have one.
Hope you have fun at camp. Love, Sarah
  P.S. please write me back, I love you.

Here I am, filling pages and pages with longing for her body.

. . .

Sarah slept like a windmill; her legs and arms kicking and tossing the covers as she dreamed. I refused to share a bed with her. She had small hands and bit her nails obsessively until she started wearing fake ones: long, plastic things that made it difficult for her to text. She liked it when I made her fly; I lay on my back and tucked my feet just

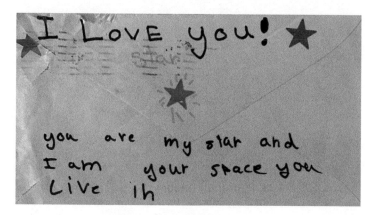

A letter to Tess

under her rib cage, lifting her body with my outstretched legs until we reached one perfect moment of balance.

She broke her nose when she was seven, playing near the pool at my stepmother's house. There was no railing on the surrounding porch, just a drop-off to earth and trees. I was standing near the house, watching her run laps around the pool, when she tripped and flew off the deck. I saw her small body hang in midair for half a breath and then heard the resounding thud as she hit the ground. I was in shock, couldn't make my feet move toward her.

My stepmother, normally slow due to the effects of chronic Lyme disease, raced off the deck and down toward my sister. She carried Sarah up to the house and laid her

on the kitchen table. Her face was covered in dirt and blood. Her nose looked like misshapen putty, and I could see packed earth in her nostrils. I felt myself growing faint, ears ringing, eyes blurring. As I wobbled toward the floor, my sister sat up and grabbed my hand. "I'm going to be okay, sissy." I can't help but wonder if it was moments like this that convinced Sarah that I could not help her when she was hurting, that taught her she would have to take care of me even when she was in trouble.

Here I am, still looking for her help.

The Beginning

Every time we made a lap around the hospital, we stopped at the delivery room. The door swung open, and I could hear my mother's insistent breath, her wails of pain. When I looked in, her face was red and wet and she was clutching the arm of my father. I was five, on the verge of six, when my sister was born. A friend of my parents walked me around the hospital while we waited for Sarah to arrive. This is different from my own beginning. My father was not there. I came into the world and settled in my mother's arms.

On the day Sarah was born, our father was there, but there was also a problem. I was too young at the time to fully understand, but I remember the panicked look on the nurses' faces and the persistent paging of a doctor. Sarah's head had emerged, but her shoulder had lodged behind my mother's pubic bone. She was, as she would spend much of her life, stuck. The doctor was brought in to put his hand inside my mother and ease my sister out. Before he could do so, in a room full of anxious hospital staff, my sister shifted her shoulder and without any help was born.

When my father handed her to me, I stared at the strange, beautiful thing in my young arms, and I thought she was tough. I wasn't tough. I liked making magic potions in the backyard and cried when our older half brother, Jed, told me that the lizard near my foot was a baby alligator. My father's raised voice scared me. I had a recurring dream that I would fall out of my bed and never land. I would fall, arm outstretched into utter darkness, until I woke up, terrified. At night, I had to imagine that a large wolf carried me on her back into the Kingdom of Dreams in order to fall asleep. I was unsettled and sensitive, and my sister was strong and wily.

We shared a room when we were young. Two twin-size beds, a dresser, and stacks of plastic crates filled with books. Sarah liked to watch me clean the room, and since I was older, the task fell mostly to me. Once I was finished, if I left for more than a few minutes, I came back to a hurricane of blankets, books, and toys. Sometimes I yelled at her or pinched her little arms. There were days, though, that I announced that the floor had turned to deadly lava because of her bad behavior. We leaped to the safety of our beds. We coaxed each other to venture into the hot molten carpet and retrieve necessary items for survival, making death-defying leaps from the bed to a piece of clothing crumpled on the floor.

At night, we lay in our twin beds and whispered to each other. Now, when I am trying to fall asleep, I try to recall what her voice sounded like. For a moment I have it, and then, much like trying to remember a dream upon waking, it slips away from me. In my dreams, she speaks to me, but I never hear her voice.

I liked to stick my hand under her pillow at night and poke her just as she was falling asleep. I quietly slipped my hand under her pillow and taunted her, making my fingers dance under her head. She jerked out of almost-sleep and told me, "Stop it, sissy." Quickly, I pulled my hand back and held it up as evidence of my innocence.

"It's probably a monster," I said, listening to her breathe next to me, feeling the hesitation of her belief.

Homes

Before Sarah was born, my mother would wake me up some nights so we could look for my father. She would bundle me up, carry me through the chilly night air, and buckle me into our old Chevy. We would drive around to cheap hotels to see if we could spot his Crayola-blue Toyota truck in the parking lot. I would scan the rows of cars until I found the color blue to point out to my mom. Sometimes we found him at three in the morning, his beat-up truck tucked in the back of a Motel 6. I know this happened several times, but I have no recollection of what happened once the truck was found. All that remains is my mother and me, driving in the dark, looking for his betrayal.

My mother was an artist, finishing up her master's in painting while I was still in preschool. She would bring me to her drawing classes. I have memories of the smell of charcoal, bodies draped over chairs, the sound of large pieces of paper rustling. She had to bring me with her, since my father wasn't able to watch me. He was either working on a construction crew he would inevitably bail on, or at home, watching TV while chain-smoking. My mother finished her degree, defended her thesis while pregnant with my sister. She has never stopped painting.

My father wanted to be a writer. He wrote a science fiction book before I was born. One of his female protagonists was named Soanna, and within the world he had created, she was considered the perfect woman. When I was born, Soanna became my middle name. I never read that book, or any others he wrote. I believe my father had an agent once, who tried to sell his nonfiction book about his years of involvement in Native American shamanism. The rights were sold to a small publishing house in France. That was the extent of my father's imprint on the literary world.

. . .

My uncle Rex once told me a story about a time he visited our house. I was five years old, and Rex was watching *Sesame Street* with me while my parents were out. He described the sounds of my parents' car screeching into the driveway, their loud voices as they stomped up the stairs, the slamming of the front door so hard the house shook, and my mother and father retreating to their bedroom to continue their fight. Once my parents were sequestered in their room, I turned to Rex with a somber look on my face and said, "They are going to have some alone time now," before turning my gaze back to the TV, the roar of their anger in the background.

My parents split when I was ten and my sister was four. They found new partners quickly. My mother's new boyfriend, Rick, was introduced to my sister and me one evening over dinner. He moved in later that night. My father drove us to meet his partner, a woman named Sharon, and didn't inform us beforehand that she was the person he'd had an affair with years before, causing my parents' first major separation.

Rick admired Captain von Trapp from *The Sound of Music*, before Maria comes along. He was an acclaimed nonviolent peace activist who went to prison for a year after a demonstration had gone awry. He drove a VW van that had a distinct sputter and owned a sweet, old pit bull named Hobo. He liked to sea-kayak, protest, and drink. It was clear from the first night that I met Rick that I wasn't going to like the change in our household. My mother was an artist who slept in late and was lax about housework and playtime, whereas Rick preferred order, cleanliness, and discipline. My mother liked that Rick was organized where she was messy, that he was focused where she was distracted. He said he was going to get a whistle so he could summon Sarah and me.

Sharon was the antithesis of Rick. She was warm, funny, and wickedly smart. Our first night meeting her, she grilled salmon, played Nina Simone while we ate, and taught my sister and me all the good hiding spots in her house so we could scare each other. By the time Sarah and I figured out who she was, the woman our father had left our mother for years before, it was too late—we already loved her.

Sharon had chronic Lyme disease and an accompanying myriad of health issues. Her knees would swell to the size of grapefruits, and she spent a lot of time in pain. That meant she spent a lot of time at home, and a lot of that time was spent reading: Arundhati Roy, Jonathan Carroll, Toni Morrison. She lived in the mountains, a half-hour drive away from the highway. She and her former partner, Shelly, had built the house together in the early 1970s. Sharon liked to tell stories of the two of them carrying the heavy wooden beams up the hill, when they measured something wrong and everything was crooked, how for the first few years their roof was a tarp. Sharon's friends were mostly queer, primarily sober, and they had all known one another for decades. They were loud and told great stories while everyone drank diet sodas and smoked cigarettes on the porch overlooking the hillside.

Sharon had been the caretaker for both her parents, her grandmother, and countless friends, many who had died during the AIDS epidemic. For as long as I've known her, death has followed her closely, with a remarkable number of people dying on or within days of her May birthday. She said she was cursed. The curse didn't seem to affect her ability to love or be vulnerable, though. Sharon was frank: about sobriety, sexuality, death, and her history.

. . .

As Sarah entered kindergarten and I hit puberty, we lived in these two very different homes. My father's house, where he lay on the couch, his T-shirt riding up his expanding belly, chain-smoking and watching football, while Sharon splashed with us in her pool and answered our questions about everything: being queer, falling in love, sex, what it meant to be a good friend. And my mother's house, where she read out loud to us and came to every swim meet, but was partnered to a man who was cruel and impossible to please.

If I could go back in time, I would take my mother's hand and tell her, "Pick a man as wild and absolute as your paintings. You are worthy of unwavering kindness." I would whisper in Sharon's ear, "Don't return to my father—he will apologize to you for eight hours the day he wins you back, and then you will never hear him say 'I'm sorry' again." But as a child, it seemed normal to me that my mothers would choose such men as their partners. It did not occur to me that both of these women deserved better until I was much older.

When Sarah was just six years old, she told me that Rick was an alcoholic. I wasn't even sure she knew what that word meant until she showed me his secret stash of beer bottle caps. She was also scared of our father, wary of

his moods and quick to lie to him if she thought it could get her out of trouble. But she was fast to forgive both of them as well. She wanted a father, even if that father was a drunk or mean or didn't pay enough attention to her. She wanted to be loved.

Excuse Me, Mr. President

Rick was a well-known and revered activist, lauded for his peaceful but persistent approach to environmental and antinuclear issues. He was mildly famous within progressive circles, in large part because of an incident involving a crystal eagle and Ronald Reagan that landed him in prison. In the early 1990s Rick founded the Hundredth Monkey Project, a series of concerts and demonstrations to bring together antinuclear activists. In 1992 a few thousand people gathered in Nevada near the nuclear test site for a weekend of activism. On the final day of the event, many of those involved traveled to Las Vegas to hold a demonstration outside the Department of Energy's office.

That same day, Rick, using a borrowed press pass, was allowed into a luncheon honoring Ronald Reagan. The former president had been presented with a large crystal eagle and was speaking to a room full of his devotees, the

National Association of Broadcasters, who had awarded him with the statue. Rick snuck onto the stage, smashed the thirty-pound eagle, and stepped forward to the microphone, saying, "Excuse me, President Reagan." He had planned to give an impassioned speech against nuclear testing, but instead half a dozen Secret Service men tackled him, while more whisked Reagan away to safety. In the video of the event, still available to watch on YouTube, the shards of crystal look like shrapnel as they fly over the former president's head. Reagan was not harmed, but Rick, after various legal battles, was sentenced to around a year in prison and ordered to pay a $2,000 fine, cementing his status as a hero to the cause.

One morning, when I was fifteen years old, Rick threw a heavy wooden chair at my head because I had failed to clean up the cream cheese from my breakfast. The chair missed, crashing into the wall beside me and cracking into two pieces. He berated me as I shut my eyes and hoped my car pool to school, which was honking a friendly hello from our driveway, couldn't hear his threats.

Rick was, privately, a terrible alcoholic who was emotionally abusive to me, my sister, and my mom. My mother did not know this when they first got together. He didn't drink in front of us initially, though it's hard to remember when that changed. I do remember when my mother found hundreds and hundreds of bottles and cans hidden inside the walls of our garage, and when Sarah, six years old, dumped out a backpack full of beer bottle caps onto Sharon's table and said, "See, I told you he drinks a lot." Eventually his alcoholism and anger lived openly with us all the time.

There was often the threat of violence, the hint that his rage could turn into something more. When Rick was angry with my sister, he would grab her arms or neck but let go just before bruises formed. He left marks on the walls from throwing plates laden with food when he was upset. It filled our house, this hurricane of anger, but he was careful not to let it touch us hard enough to leave physical marks. Still, he would destroy a shelf in a frenzy if he bumped against it one too many times, take a hammer to it, screaming, and reduce it to splinters while we hid in our rooms until his mood had passed.

I vacillated between blaming my mom for allowing this man into our home and feeling sorry for her. She tried to integrate him into our family, even had us go to family therapy, which promptly went awry when the therapist asked me how I felt about my stepdad, and I said, in front of Rick, "I hate him."

"Any other feelings?" she asked.

"Nope, I really just hate him," I replied.

My hatred spilled over to my mother too. I once threw an entire drawer of silverware at her in a rage over Rick's presence. Her most common response to Sarah or me when we asked her why she stayed with him was "I love him." But *why* did she love him? I didn't understand the trauma that had led her heart to him, how she had found a man like her own father: cold, critical, and withholding of praise. I didn't understand until I made similar choices.

· · ·

Rick suffered from depression and spoke often of suicide. He made attempts at emotional growth. He joined a men's group where guys beat drums around a firepit and talked about masculinity, and he tried family counseling on occasion. He attended AA on and off for years. His coping skills, however, seemed fairly limited to drinking and passing on the abuse he himself had faced. I believe that he thought love and respect were the offspring of fear. He used to say he wished he could take a pill and, *poof*, disappear from everyone's memory.

Where the physical violence managed to just miss us, the emotional abuse hit its targets squarely. When my sister and I began to develop breasts and butts, Rick routinely called us fat and lazy, looking away from our curves, as though uncomfortable with pubescent bodies. His nickname for my sister was Piggy. When he and my mom fought, he attacked her weight and accused her of setting a poor example for us because she wasn't thin enough. He disliked when one of us talked about something he didn't understand. He had not gone to college and got upset when he felt his intelligence was challenged. He routinely called us "spoiled American brats" despite the fact that we lived off my mother's artist-in-residency stipend and a little help from my grandmother. He said to my mom, "Everything would be great if you just did exactly as I said all the time."

He had strange restrictions around food. When I was a teenager, he started buying hundred-pound bags of oatmeal and insisted we eat it for breakfast every day until the bag was empty. He once made my sister eat cereal with orange juice because we were out of soy milk. He discouraged us from consuming dairy but ate pints of Ben & Jerry's himself. Regularly, he took everything that was nearing expiration or growing mold and chopped it all up to scramble with eggs, calling it "Rick's Special." He viewed food waste as the pinnacle of what was wrong with Americans.

The rule was that if Sarah and I didn't clean up our things, he might throw them away to "teach us a lesson." In some of Rick's rarer moods, he dictated how often we could shower and for how long. Hygiene, clothing, weight, all these were things he felt it was his job to have a say in. There was no such thing as privacy in our house.

Sarah and I became allies. We traded food that we weren't supposed to eat: candy, salty snacks, sugary drinks. If I wanted privacy while talking on the phone, Sarah would ask Rick to show her something in the garden or his garage workshop. If Sarah broke something, we would try to fix it or smuggle it out of the house before he saw. Rick didn't like it when I read too much; I think my intellect bothered him. So Sarah would play quietly in my room while I read, letting me know when Rick was on his way to my door so I could slip my book under the covers and pretend to be playing with her. We learned to hide things, to speak in code with friends on the phone, to read the room for his moods. I snuck in showers at other people's houses. I felt like I didn't have ownership over my things or my body; everything could be taken away or denied if Rick was angry.

My mother once lit Rick's bike on fire. When she couldn't get the fire to start, I was the one who handed her a container of lighter fluid from the garage. She had found out he was cheating. Her first response was to throw rocks at the woman's house, aiming for the windows, while Rick sat inside. When that proved unsatisfactory, she drove furiously home and set aflame the bike and cart he had used to travel across the country multiple times, one of his favorite things. My mom, Sarah, and I stood in the driveway while it burned, watching the dark smoke drift toward the bay.

I can still remember her face, angry but satisfied, her blue eyes turning a steely gray.

My mother left Rick permanently in 2006. The last thing he ever said to me, at the end of a screaming fight when I was close to twenty years old (still a few years before he and my mother split for good), was that one day I would come find him and thank him for how he parented me. In 2010 Rick married a woman in front of a small group of family and friends. Two weeks later, he woke up and shot himself in the head.

Good Kind

Typing on my family computer one day, just a few months out of high school, I rested my hand on the curve of my neck. My thumb brushed over two small lumps that I had never noticed before. I tried to tell myself that they were swollen glands, a result of an infection or a small cold, but when I pressed my fingers to them, I felt uneasy; they were rubbery and floated almost gracefully, not like any swollen lymph node I had encountered before. I got up and walked into the living room, looked at my mom and sister, and said, "I think I have cancer." They looked up from the couch and laughed, and my mom sort of grimaced, as if to say *That's ridiculous.* I laughed, too, but I went into the other room and made an appointment.

I went to the local health clinic. The nurse practitioner felt my neck and took my temperature, which was elevated. "This is nothing to worry about," she said. "Just swollen glands because you have an infection right now." She wrote out a prescription and handed it to me. "Take these antibiotics for seven days, and if nothing changes, come back to see me." She turned to leave. "Of course, there's a small chance that it's cancer, but don't worry, even if it is, it's the good kind." With that, she left the room.

The good kind, I thought.

Seven days later, I was back. "Hmm, let's see, so the antibiotics didn't help?" she asked, pushing her slipping glasses back up her nose.

"Nope," I said. "I mean, I don't have a sore throat anymore, but these lumps are still here." She called in another nurse, who was short, needing to stand on her tiptoes to feel my neck.

"Cat scratch fever," she said expertly, nodding her head.

"Of course," said the other nurse. "I should have thought of that myself." She wrote me another prescription. "Take these antibiotics for seven days. If nothing changes, come back to see me."

I changed doctors and moved to a private practice. Dr. Baschill was an immediately comforting presence. When she entered the small exam room, she smiled at my tired face. "Don't worry," she said. "Whatever this is, I am going to make sure you get the best care." She was honest with me. Lumps like these could mean any number of things: mono, HIV, an infection, cancer. She was firm in her belief that cancer or HIV was a very small possibility, but "I want you to know all the things you could be up against." After running test after test, she called me into her office. She sat across from me. "Rose," she said simply, "I think it's time you see a surgeon." She took my hand into hers; it was cool against my flushed skin. "You will be fine," she told me. "No matter what happens, you will be fine."

I made light of all this to my friends and family. "The good kind," I said, reassuring them that the worst-case scenario wasn't "that bad." I jokingly referred to my swollen glands as my "cancer lumps," and that made my friends laugh. My family stood at a distance from the possibilities. My mom was concerned but quiet. Sharon was sure I had mono. Over the phone, I could hear her softly inhaling cigarettes as she asked, again and again, "Are you sure it's not just a virus?" I wanted to take the cigarette out of her hand and place her soft fingers where my pulse should be, so she could feel the unsettling beat of my tumors.

Dr. Baschill sent me to Dr. Cobb, a surgeon. Dr. Cobb played the piano. He had a daughter who was almost my age. He played classical music at concerts to raise money for local charities. I liked him for all of these reasons. I sat very still when he showed me a large, glistening needle and explained that he would biopsy my lymph node to see if there was cancerous material present. Over the next few days I ignored the bruise forming around my collarbone and pretended everything was normal; I kissed a blond-haired boy, I drank rum until three and secretly longed to be in college.

Dr. Cobb called me in to tell me that the results were "inconclusive but suspicious." I would need to have a surgical biopsy. I relayed this information back to my loved ones casually. Sarah was twelve years old and hadn't quite reached the stage when her baby fat had melted away, and she perpetually had a boyfriend. She didn't say much when I told her because the word *biopsy* didn't mean anything to her.

The biopsy was scheduled quickly. I liked the antianxiety drugs they gave me when I came in for the surgery. I was suddenly and utterly free from the hidden worry I had been holding in my chest. When the nurses wheeled me through two swinging doors to the operating room, I laughed at the "Booty Free" sign overhead, even after one nurse pointed to the soft slippers he had to remove from his feet before entering the operating room. Everyone kept telling me to relax. I counted down, just like they told me to: 10 . . . 9 . . . 8 . . . 7 . . . After the surgery, no one said anything to me as I was wheeled back through the swinging doors. Still under the fog of anesthetic, I overheard the doctor tell my mother that I had cancer.

The pamphlet they gave me at the hospital, *Understand Your Illness!*, told me I was diagnosed with Hodgkin's lymphoma, a cancer of the lymphatic system. As Hodgkin's disease progresses, it compromises the body's ability to fight infection. Hodgkin's is fairly rare; only about 7,000 people in the United States are diagnosed every year. It is not to be confused with non-Hodgkin's lymphoma, which affects about 66,000 people per year and has a much higher mortality rate. I was told repeatedly by my doctors that I was lucky to have been diagnosed with the rarer form.

With treatment, I had a 90 percent chance of living. I had a 10 percent chance of not making it to my twenty-first birthday or going to college or growing old. If I did not start treatment, I would be dead in a year. No percentages were used when explaining this to me; I *would* be dead in a year without treatment.

I cried only twice in front of the doctors: when they told me I would lose all my hair, and when they told me I would have to defer college for a year. I did not cry when they told me that I would go through chemotherapy and radiation. I would need to have a port catheter put into my chest, under my skin, sitting just below my clavicle, which would be removed after chemo was over. I had no idea what any of this was, so I just nodded. Sharon told me to start taking a pad of paper with a list of questions already written down and to take notes on what they told me.

· · ·

My whole life became about being ill. My calendar diminished to only doctors' appointments. I went to chemo, and my friends went to keggers. I listened to their hungover talk of raging parties and freshman math classes while I sat, a sickly yellow from the Adriamycin the oncology nurse had pumped into my chest the day before. My boyfriend, Phillip, worked in the late afternoons at the local Indian casino until almost midnight and worked out at the gym during the day for at least two hours. On his days off, he liked drinking with the boys and drunk-dialing me while I slept off the previous day's treatment.

I was put on a chemotherapy regimen referred to as ABVD (Adriamycin, bleomycin, vinblastine, dacarbazine), the first line of treatment for Hodgkin's lymphoma. I received my treatment at a private practice about twenty minutes from my home, run by a group of oncologists. My doctor, Dr. Bonis, was a tall, balding man who liked to tell me about his other Hodgkin's patient, a young woman, not too much older than me, who was "regrettably" dying. She was not responding to treatment, the ABVD that I was also receiving.

My chemo happened in a small room with nine chairs for patients. My favorite chair was the blue plaid recliner. It sat in the middle of the room, not too close to the door, which when opened carried a draft, nor too far away from the bathroom, which was important when you had to drag an IV stand in with you. Everyone else getting treatment was at least twenty years older than me. During one of my first appointments, I sat down and an older man leaned over to me. With a kind smile, he informed me that I was sitting in a chair reserved for cancer patients. He looked unbearably sad when I explained that I was there for treatment.

Sharon took me to these appointments. She packed a bucket, blankets, and water for the twenty-minute drive home afterward, in case I became nauseated. To administer the chemo drugs, a nurse would numb the skin over my port, a small device surgically installed under my skin and connected to a vein. The nurse would then take a small fishhook-like needle and attach it to a catheter just below my scarred skin. The first thing injected into the port was an antianxiety drug and an antinausea drug that I lovingly called the "ants in the pants" drugs because for roughly thirty seconds after they were administered, it felt as if my behind was on fire. The antianxiety drug caused me to feel weightless.

About an hour into my treatment, I would look down at my hands, now the sickly shade of a bruised banana. I was not sure exactly which of the drugs did this, but it was the thing I noticed first. When it happened, I knew I would be able to keep my eyes open for only a short time before nodding off in the recliner.

When I went, I went quickly, nearly comatose. My head would drop to my chest. That was when I began to remember. In my chemical-laced dreams, I floated from memory to memory. I remembered red brushstrokes, pumpkins in October, burning my finger by touching a lit match when I was four, lighting lanterns and floating them in a pond. I remembered stars, being late to school so often that the school sent home a notice to my mom, pancakes and eggs when we went camping, the quilt with rabbits on it, watching beauty pageants in the dark, eating popcorn made in a wok. I remembered my mother. I dreamed of my father as a cowboy, before I was born, and saw him riding on a chocolate-brown horse through the desert. When I woke up, I staggered to Sharon's car, and she drove me home while I nodded in and out of consciousness in the back seat.

After my third chemotherapy appointment, I was told the treatment was working and my tumors were shrinking. I would live. The year went on: doctors, dreaming, jaundice, needles, loneliness.

. . .

On Sarah's twelfth birthday, a bunch of friends and family got together to celebrate. One of my parents' friends, whom I hadn't seen since I was diagnosed, handed me a small wrapped gift and card. As I sat down to unwrap the present, I heard a cry of outrage and looked over to see Sarah, surrounded by gifts, with an indignant look, clearly unhappy that I had received something on her birthday. "Oh my god," she exclaimed, "when it's your birthday, it will be your birthday AND you'll have cancer!" Everyone laughed at her vexed young face.

On my nineteenth birthday I was fitted for a radiation mask, a plastic mesh screen molded perfectly to my face. When getting radiation, I would have to lay flat on my back, my arms and legs strapped down so that I couldn't move. I had to be completely still; they bolted the mask to the table so that my head would be immobile. It was the only treatment-related appointment I cried through. I thought the technicians couldn't see my tears through the mask, but one of them squeezed my hand, just for a moment. I went to a yoga class in the afternoon, designed for people who were sick or elderly, and walked out to find a parking ticket on my car. I hoped the day would get better. It was my birthday AND I had cancer.

My boyfriend Phillip's mother had died a few years earlier, and he informed me on the evening of my birthday that it was also the anniversary of her death. We spent the night talking about his mom. He fell asleep still in his clothes. I stayed up, remembering the sound of the mask being bolted down. Months later, I would find the invitation to her memorial while organizing papers in our spare room. Phillip's mother had actually died weeks after my birthday. He had merged us, his dead mother and his sick girlfriend; he had given me flowers on Mother's Day. When I showed him the invitation I had found, he wept until my shoulder was wet. We never talked about it again.

. . .

I made Sarah and Tess come to one of my radiation appointments so that they could better understand what having cancer meant. They pressed their faces into the glass that separated them from the room where I received treatment. No one could be in the room with me when the radiation machine was on; it was too dangerous. Out of the corner of my eye, I could see Sarah's face turn serious when my mask went on and I was secured to the table. Next, lead blankets were placed on various parts of my body to protect the rest of me from radiation, the parts that cancer didn't live in. After that, a large machine was lowered down and lined up perfectly with small tattoos I had received to ensure perfect placement every time.

The technicians left the room. Sarah and Tess became blurs in my periphery. The machine whirred to life, and I closed my eyes. Radiation doesn't feel like much of anything as it's happening, sometimes like an instant, stinging sunburn. It was the accumulation of radiation that was painful. That was when skin turned raw, hair fell away, sweat glands gave up. It only took a few minutes, a short burst of gamma rays to attack the bad cells that lived in my body. The good cells killed were regrettable casualties.

When the machine came to a stop, I opened my eyes and strained to see the blur of Sarah and Tess. They were gone. I found them in the hallway of the hospital, Tess holding Sarah as she cried. "I didn't know," she said through her howls, "I didn't know that's what happened to you." I knew it was a mistake, in that moment, to have tried to teach her a lesson. She was only twelve. I took her in my arms and whispered apologies into her ear until she calmed down.

. . .

Within a few months, there were no signs of Hodgkin's anymore. In five years, I would be told I was officially cancer-free. My body was never the same. I still do not sweat out of my right armpit. When I get a massage near my lymph nodes, I become ill, feverish, and clammy from released chemotherapy drugs still stored in my body. I am at high risk for breast cancer, the radiation I received having damaged the tissue. I have two scars that will never go away.

Sarah and I were never quite the same, either. I left home just as she went through puberty. I do not know when she first got her period or had her first kiss. There is a betrayal there, to not have been beside her as her body changed. I think of her pressing her face against the glass of my treatment room. We had been allies in our home, and then we faced our own wars alone. We would never live in the same house again. The thing we most often said to each other was "You don't know me anymore."

Entry Points

The first night I drank was also the first night I had sex. I was on a high school trip in China, where we were touring Bertolt Brecht's play *The Caucasian Chalk Circle*. I was seventeen and a senior. I went to an unusual high school: a performing arts charter school with a total of ten students. Since I had spent the better part of the last six years around Rick, I had never been interested in drinking. I associated it with hidden piles of beer cans, his hairy body passed out in the driveway on the night of my mom's art opening, the slur of his voice as he yelled at me to clean up the goddamn kitchen. In China I watched as my classmates drank wine with scorpions curled up in the bottom of the bottle. I laughed as they kissed and danced and threw up over the side of the boat, but I did not participate.

On our last night, in Beijing, we went to a restaurant that turned into a club after ten. The tables were cleared, and patrons climbed on top of them to dance and drink. At the bar, I asked for a tequila sunrise because I had seen someone order it on TV once. It was sweet, citrusy, and ended with a wild kick to my throat that made me feel invincible.

I walked home with classmates barefoot through the streets of Beijing. I flashed a passing cab and laughed, giving no thought to my chubby, white stomach. I went up to a sophomore's room and had sex for the first time. It was, unsurprisingly, awful. My body was numb and wobbly. I gave him sloppy kisses and told him to put it in. He was equally drunk and obliged. All the while we could hear our classmates giggling outside the door. I remember a pinch, a dry attempt at movement, and then sleep.

· · ·

I don't know the first night Sarah drank. The first night I caught her, she was fourteen years old and had a group of girls sleeping over. I walked in on one of them vomiting out of Sarah's bedroom window.

"So, you guys are drunk," I said.

"No, we aren't!" my sister shrieked as her friend pulled her head out of the window, wiping her mouth clean.

"Yeah, you are. And"—I made a show of sniffing the air—"it's Bacardi 151."

My sister's mouth dropped open, and then she smiled sheepishly. "Okay, yeah. Don't tell Mom," she begged.

I didn't.

· · ·

I remember when I was home visiting from college and saw her getting out of the bath. She was fourteen, and I caught a glimpse of her shaved pubic area while I was brushing my teeth. I realized then that she might be having sex, that her body was no longer something I knew anything about. I found out later that the first time she had sex, she was thirteen. My dad let her and a seventeen-year-old boy named Gil sleep in a tent together, alone, at my dad's property in the mountains. Where was I when my sister was deciding to open her body to someone? Where was I to talk to her afterward?

I imagine two movie screens running next to each other, our lives side by side. There are places where the images are the same: the night we did coke and I threw up into the bathroom sink (all I could say was "I'm so sorry, I'm so sorry" as she cleaned vomit from my hair); the weekend she made her amends to me at a women's sober-living house; the day our father died. There is much of her screen that is blank for me, that I have attempted to fill in with journals, conversations, and investigation. In those dark gaps of her life, I imagine great shadowy monsters I could have saved her from. In every version, it is my fault.

Sarah loved boys and girls. Sarah loved kissing and drama and shitty sex. She loved commitment and cheating and fights with girls she called sluts for sleeping with strung-out boys she had claimed for herself. She was suspended from high school for making out with a girl on

campus. She moved her first serious boyfriend, Ethan, into my mother's house, threatening to run away if my mom didn't let him stay. She would fuck this boyfriend in the farmhouse my mom was restoring. My mother and I would sit at the dining room table watching the old chandelier tremble and sway, small bits of dust and plaster falling down on us until the noise of a high-pitched moan would carry down the stairs and all would go quiet.

After I left home, Sarah and my mom fought all the time, about her cutting class or Ethan living at the house. They had a similar temper, quick to explode and quick to forgive. My attempts at playing peacemaker were met with annoyance, although I was often the first one either of them reached out to when they were fighting. It was not uncommon for one of them to call me "condescending," probably because I relished telling each of them what they were doing wrong. I felt both invulnerable after beating cancer and convinced I was going to die young anyway. I had the answers for every question except my own.

My mother called me in my first semester at college. Sarah was skipping school, not doing her homework, and my mother said she was "at her wit's end." I called Sarah as I walked to class, trudging slowly up a steep hill. I tried to convey all nineteen years of my wisdom to Sarah. "You really need to get your shit together—Mom is pissed, and I am tired of hearing about it."

"You have no idea what my life is like," Sarah said. "And Mom is super hard to live with."

"Why? Because she makes you go to school?" I sighed. "You're such a fucking drama queen."

"It's really hard going to school where everyone knows what a perfect student you were." She was near tears, but she said the word *perfect* like it was burning the inside of her mouth. "It's a lot to live up to."

"So now it's my fault that you aren't doing your homework?"

"That's not what—"

"Everything would be so much better if you just did exactly what I said."

If I could, I would pause both of our stories, with me figuring out my life after cancer, and her on the verge of fifteen and her first encounter with opiates. I would go to her and lay my head in her lap and tell her how scared I was of the cancer returning to my body. I would ask her about Ethan and school. She would tell me the things that I'd only discover once it was already too late: she and Ethan did small lines of coke in her room, drank from hidden bottles of cheap vodka and rum, crushed up Adderall and snorted until their noses bled. She would tell me how she ran through the redwoods drunk, smoking pot out of an apple pipe, how she hated

With Tess

her stomach so much the diet pills seemed the only way forward. I would listen.

. . .

Instead, I went to Rome to celebrate finishing my cancer treatment and spent two months drinking, dancing, fucking, and feeling invincible before heading to school. Sarah met Tyson and OxyContin.

Opioids 101

Tomorrow I go home. Tyson said he got me a present, and then I asked what it was. It's oxy. What is he thinking? Like yeah, I do want it and it will be fun . . . but after everything I said about wanting to get my life together, about wanting to stay sober, why would he tempt me like that? Does he really want to have that shit in my body? Does he want me to be sober or a drug addict?

—*Sarah's journal, January 10, 2007*

The first time I took an opioid was when I was prescribed Vicodin following my surgical biopsy. I threw up for hours, a green foul bile that was thick and viscous. A bitter taste coated my tongue that I will forever associate with painkillers.

There is technically a distinction between opiates and opioids, or at least there used to be. Opiates are drugs derived from the opium poppy plant, like heroin. Opioids are drugs made in a lab using the same chemical structure as opiates and mimicking their effects, like oxycodone. The term *opioid* now refers to both. Opioids are typically used to treat pain but also produce a sense of well-being or euphoria. Opioids bind to and stimulate opioid receptors in the body. When they attach to the receptors, they can block pain signals your brain is sending to your body. They also release large amounts of dopamine, which can make a person feel relaxed, happy, and high.

Prescription opioids include codeine, hydrocodone (Vicodin), morphine, oxycodone (OxyContin, Percocet), hydromorphone (Dilaudid), and fentanyl. Sarah told me that when she first tried OxyContin, she didn't know that it was akin to prescription heroin. It was just a pill that made her body feel good and her brain feel happy. She was fifteen when she first took oxy, and within a year she would be smoking it because it brought the high on more quickly.

. . .

What we now call the opioid crisis started in the 1980s, when several respected medical journals released articles that downplayed the negative and addictive aspects of prescribing opioids for chronic pain. In the 1990s the pharmaceutical industry (and in particular the company Purdue Pharma) took advantage of these claims and began aggressively marketing opioids, chiefly OxyContin.

Purdue Pharma pleaded guilty in 2007 to fraudulently misbranding OxyContin—the company had asserted that oxycodone was less addictive than other opioids on the market. Purdue had even persuaded the FDA to place a label on the packaging claiming that the delayed absorption of the pill was believed to reduce the likelihood of misuse. In 2001 this label was removed from the packaging, and no opioid has since received one.

Between 1996 and 2001, the number of OxyContin prescriptions in the United States grew from 300,000 to 6 million. Research says that 20 to 30 percent of chronic pain patients prescribed opiates will misuse them. About 80 percent of people who use heroin begin by first abusing prescription opioids.

Sarah turned to heroin because oxy was too expensive, and she was using too much to be able to afford it anymore. She liked heroin because it made her feel like nothing could touch her. She could disconnect from her bad feelings, the shame that gnawed at her, the lack of control she had in her day-to-day life. The original point, she told me, was to feel good. And then it became about not feeling bad, about avoiding the pain of withdrawal and the deep, unending depression that took over when she tried to get clean.

Various doctors have tried to prescribe me different opiates following other surgeries, but after a couple more times trying to take them with the same results, I began listing opiates as an allergy. Because of this, I have never smoked opium or tried heroin. Sarah did not have the same aversion.

Inherit

My mother taught me to love sardines and mystery books. She was the first person to tell me I could be anything I wanted. When I was a child, I would press my ear to her stomach, imagining she was teaching me a new language with every murmur and breath. She was steadfastly present, but emotionally unpredictable. Her nickname for me as a child was Queen Bee. She lives in a beautiful farmhouse, the acres in the back inhabited by her cows, donkeys, and goats. She is a successful painter, an animal rights activist, and eerily intuitive.

She likes to tell the story of how she wore skirts so short in high school, she had to wear bathing suit bottoms underneath. She was the kind of mom who periodically suggested I stay home from school, play hooky, and spend the day together. She taught me to read by having us alternate reading pages out loud before bed. In first grade, I was caught kissing a girl at a sleepover at a friend's house.

Her mother was furious, and I was sure my parents would be equally upset. When I got home, my mother took me aside and told me it was no big deal. "Kiss whoever you like," she said. "But maybe wait until you are a little older."

We once convinced Sarah that there was elf blood in our family, a Scandinavian lineage of magic that Sarah would only know the secrets of when she turned sixteen. For years, Sarah would pull me aside and ask if we were just messing with her or if she was really going to inherit powers when she got older. This story still makes my mother laugh. When a hunter wouldn't stop shooting ducks at the edges of the bay, right by our front yard, my mother egged the inside of his truck; he never came back.

. . .

My mother can be generous, and she can be hard to communicate with. I vacillate between feeling like I am a great daughter or a terrible one. I wish I could divine the secret to our relationship, a hymn that could translate our misunderstandings into something more poetic than irritated texts or hurt feelings. I can't tell if we are too alike or too different. We both dance in supermarkets, weep while watching most movies, and love puzzles. I tend to hold on to feelings and want to talk things out, exhaustively, at times. My mother sends me articles with the title "Do You Cry Too Much? You May Be a 'Highly Sensitive Person.'" She prefers to hug and let go, with little desire to dissect whatever argument happened.

I am often caught unawares when I have hurt my mother's feelings. It is never what I think it will be. She will isolate herself from me at these times, disappear from text, phone, or email. Months can go by, and I will only know she is ready to talk because she sends me an emoji with no inherent meaning—a panda, the Swedish flag, a bug. That is my cue to connect.

. . .

When I was ten years old, I was asked to read a poem I had written in front of the other fourth- and fifth-grade students, our parents, and the teachers. A few other students were also asked to perform or read. The few of us that were asked to participate talked after class and discussed how embarrassing it would be to have our parents there. When I went home after school, I informed my mother that she was not allowed to come. She tried to sway me by promising to stand in the back, but I didn't budge; I told her I didn't want her there.

When the day came for the performance, I stood up to read my poem and saw that everyone else's parents were there. Every single one of them. I realized, as I looked out over all the beaming, proud parents, that something had gone terribly wrong. That I had done something wrong. That I had let down my mom. I think some part of me is always afraid I have failed my parents. When I told this story to my mother, when I was an adult, she had none of the emotional attachment to it that I did. "I think I came anyway," she said, shrugging. "And just didn't tell you."

Kind of Man

I was confused for many years about the kind of man my father was, in large part because when he was with my stepmother, it was easy to attribute the positive experiences Sarah and I had at their house to both of them. Now it is easy to separate those memories and realize that *she* was the one who swam with us in the pool, and *she* was the one who organized camping trips and held my hand when I cried over my first breakup. At the time, though, after my parents split up, I felt my father's presence more than I ever had before, and I loved him for that.

My father enjoyed having a rapt audience. Having turned eleven, I was just old enough that I wanted to listen. Sarah was too young to hold his attention for long, and no matter how often she trailed behind him or broke a dish or screamed, he never gave her more than a glance or a growl. My father liked to talk, to engage, to impress, and he never was good at pretending he was interested in being around little kids. In the fight for his love, I noticeably came out on top.

This changed when my father and stepmother split up, just as I was finishing up treatment for my cancer. My father moved into a shitty one-bedroom apartment, and my stepmom stayed in the house she had built. It was a contentious split. My father told us a number of things that we found out later were lies: Sharon was having an affair with her best friend, Debbie, Sharon had taken all his money, Sharon threw him out without even a change of clothes. Shortly after, I left for a six-week celebratory postcancer backpacking trip through Italy. I left behind the rumors, the shitty apartment, my father and sister, and went to Rome to forget.

For the first time in almost twenty years my father was without a partner, girlfriend, or mistress. I think he felt unmoored in a way he hadn't felt before. Despite his charm and stories, he had been unable to fully convince the people in his life that Sharon had done the things he accused her of. Sarah had recently turned twelve; she was smart and precocious. He turned to her for comfort for the first time in her life. When I returned from my trip, their relationship looked totally different. "Your sister really saved me," he told me. "I was in a dark place, and she stuck by me." It was unsettling to come back to a completely different family dynamic. I had never seen my sister happier. She beamed when she was near our father.

She was eager to impress him, to keep his attention after he had ignored her for so long.

I was warier of my father than I had ever been. I had figured out the many lies he had told about his breakup with Sharon. I left for college, keeping him at a distance. I rarely called him or emailed. By the end of the next summer, we would be completely estranged. He lied to me about cosigning a student loan, which put my second year of college in jeopardy. In the fallout, my father hit my sister across the face. He interrogated her about me and my financial situation, and when she refused to tell him, he slapped her. I left him a voicemail telling him if he ever touched her again, I would come after him myself. He never attempted to reach out to me after that.

Sarah never stopped trying to love him. She never stopped trying to be in his life. I believe she thought she could save him, as he had told her she did when she was twelve years old.

. . .

I suppose I should have realized earlier what kind of man my father, Gary, was. He had a son, Jed, who he had abandoned when Jed was twelve. Jed would come and visit on the weekends when I was young, before Sarah was born. He was exactly what I wanted in a big brother: protective, funny, and he played terrible pranks on me that I later found hilarious. One time I was bitten by a spider, and Jed convinced four-year-old me that it was deadly. He helped me write out a will and everything. Gary was furious when he found out, but I thought it was funny. I thought everything Jed did was funny. Jed kept visiting after Sarah was born, but there are only a few pictures of him holding her when she was a baby. Soon after, Jed stopped coming on the weekends, or rather, my father stopped picking him up.

The next time I saw Jed, he was an angry seventeen-year-old. After some teenage rebellion that included crashed cars and a run-in with the police, Jed's mother called Gary and told him it was time for him to step in. Jed moved into Sharon's house, and the next few months were fraught: raised voices, Jed planting pot in the front yard, Jed blowing smoke in my face when I tried to talk to him. One night Jed chucked a heavy flashlight at Gary during a fight, in the dark, and it glanced off the side of Gary's face. After Jed's eighteenth birthday, he walked out of Gary's life for good.

Jed would eventually reconnect with Sarah and me, after he had grown up and started a family of his own. His children would run up to him and throw their arms around him. I watched at dinner as he teased them, laughed with them, and told them no when they needed to hear it. In short, he became the kind of man, the kind of father, that we all wished Gary had been. He had grown in opposition to what was modeled to him.

I only wish Sarah and I had been able to do the same.

Rome

Rome was sex on sidewalks. Rome was body shots, selling cheap tours to English speakers outside the Colosseum, and perfect cups of cappuccino sipped while standing at counters. Rome was celebrating that I hadn't died before I was twenty. Rome was blackouts, military fiancés, pub crawls in a snowstorm. Rome was trying to forget and failing. Rome was Sicily and bursting citrus trees, train rides to beaches, kissing strangers until my mouth turned raw. Rome was twice, first the summer after cancer and then again, a few years later. Rome was my first line of coke. Afterward I gave a blow job to an Italian man in a convertible and felt magnificent. Rome was pasta and cheap wine, vodka with Moroccans, waking up with no clothes on. Rome was losing euros, giving head for a bump, jumping into fountains until the Polizia showed up. Rome was Canadian au pairs and broken ribs, heatstroke, and honey from Calabria. Rome was the joke about ending up in AA, Guinness on Sundays, and internet cafés. Rome was what should have been my junior year, ignoring California and drinking my weight in cheap pub-crawl beer. Rome was not being there when my grandma or the family dog died and flying home drunk on Halloween to mourn them both. Rome was water fountains on every corner, listening to my roommate fight with her boyfriend, and peeing in the streets. Rome was magic light on ruins, riding the metro for free, and ninety-eight-proof shots that only cost two euros. Rome was the beginning of an end I vaguely intuited and tilted toward, not quite believing. The end, the end, the end rang in my ears, but for a while it sounded like possibility. I had faced cancer on my own. Beaten it on my own. I was going to college. All while my sister and mother and father lived the same day over and over again. To join them in that would be my end. The end, the end, the end hummed in my intoxicated veins. It just took a while for things to be truly over.

Lost Year

I spent two years at Sarah Lawrence before deciding to study abroad my junior year. Within a week of my Florence program starting, I was in Rome, avoiding calls from home and the school, until I was informed the embassy had listed me as a missing person. When I finally returned to Florence, I was removed from the program because of all my absences and lack of communication. The dean told me I should get on a plane and go back to Sarah Lawrence. Instead I took a train to Rome, back to the freedom of pub crawls and drinking without oversight, and moved in with two American girls and two Calabrian men.

When I returned to Sarah Lawrence a year later, I was engaged to a man stationed in Northern Italy, and once again a junior while all my friends were in their final year. I struggled when I was back: the relationship failed; I had a terrible and final phone call with my father, and then a deeply traumatic first date. I preferred to drink and do coke with strangers than deal with any of it.

And so, after barely getting through my spring semester and watching my class graduate without me, I moved home.

I moved home and drank gin and tonic, chugged bottles of Two-Buck Chuck, took shots of cheap vodka. I stole money from my mom's savings account and bought eight-balls of coke. I'd stick a dollar bill into the baggie, do my first bump in the car, and peel away from my drug dealer's house. I made sandwiches for minimum wage and showed up to work hungover, running to the back to vomit between orders. I bought coke from my sister and then lectured her about using oxy. I'd go to bars and spend most of the evening in the bathroom, doing line after line, until my heart beat erratically and my vision blurred. I'd take our town's one taxi home and give the cabdriver blow jobs, urging him to cum on my face. I still paid him for the ride, not wanting him to think I was cheap.

I'd told my mom enough about the traumatic date to explain why I needed to take time off school. I didn't tell her about the coke, the stealing, or the booze. She said she put a curse on the man and then told me she would help pay for therapy. She bought me a dog. She said I needed something to take care of.

The first therapist I went to told me she was honored by my tears. I never went back to her. My second therapist, Gaye, gently asked me if I would ever think about going to AA. Despite being drunk when she asked me, I snorted indignantly and said no. But I kept going back to her.

I threw parties in my mom's house while she was visiting Rick. I stole her debit card and bought coke for strangers. I wrote checks to myself using her checking account, and when she finally caught me, I lied and told her I had maxed out my credit cards in college and was trying to pay them back. Every week, though, I went to Gaye's office and talked, cried, tore Kleenex into tiny pieces.

. . .

The last time I had a drink was on April 15, 2008. I went out with friends for someone's birthday and finished the night doing lines by myself, in my room, and chugging beer and whiskey until I passed out. I had work the next day, a retail job I liked, a store so small only one person worked at a time. I woke up around three the next afternoon, my blankets covered in vomit, my phone blinking with messages from the owner of the store, asking why it wasn't open. My dog, Charlotte, was sitting on the bed next to me, whining softly to be let out. She had been stuck in my room with me with no food or water for hours.

I called my mom into my room. "I think I'm an alcoholic," I cried.

"I know," she said.

I called my stepmom. "I think I'm an alcoholic," I cried. Sharon had been sober for over twenty years at that point. "Can you take me to a meeting?"

"Yes," she said.

I called my boss. "I think I'm an alcoholic," I cried. "That is why I didn't open the store today. I am going to get help. I am so sorry." There was a long pause. She had someone close to her family that had struggled with drinking.

"Okay," she said. "You get one more chance."

I called my therapist. "I think I'm an alcoholic," I cried.

"Good," Gaye replied. "Now we can do some real work."

. . .

I threw up all day, until the only thing left in my body was a thick green bile that I retched from the depths of my stomach.

PART II

The Drugs

Saturday, October 19, 2013

SMALL TOWN, USA—One person was killed and another is in critical condition after a shooting incident Friday night at Little Tree Trailer Park. Sheriff's officials responded to reports of gunshots at 11:24 P.M.

Arriving officers found the two victims in different locations in the trailer park. A male victim was found deceased, his body located outside a trailer that police say was burgled. A female victim was found inside her residence.

The victims' names are not currently being released until family can be notified.

Sgt. Gerald Bickel told reporters that the victims were in a relationship but it does not appear to be a domestic dispute. "We are of the belief other individuals may have been involved." It is unclear if there are any witnesses, as Little Tree has been largely vacant the last few years.

On Saturday, investigators were at the scene continuing to collect evidence.

Any Life You Want

I pressed my thirty-day chip into the palm of her hand and told her she could have any life she wanted. We sat in my truck. She stared at the small red token I had given her. I had received it five months prior in an all-women's AA meeting I was attending regularly. I had a sponsor and was working my way through the steps.

A few months before I moved home and into the tailspin that led me to AA, Sarah had broken up with Ethan and met Tyson. Within a few weeks, Sarah was in a van full of lost boys driving to music festivals and doing ecstasy until her body's serotonin became depleted and no longer gave her the high she wanted. She looked for that feeling in other drugs: acid, alcohol, coke. She found it in OxyContin. She quickly dropped out of high school and moved away from home. Ran away, initially, and when my mom threatened to call the cops, Sarah came back and informed my mom she wasn't going to live at home anymore but would stay in the area. I think my mom was exhausted and scared, and at least this way, she would know where Sarah was.

Sarah moved to a house that was known as the Aloha House because of a giant mural painted on the side, depicting an ocean scene. It was also known for its giant parties: every drug you could want, and a particularly sketchy man named Skid who liked to touch girls after they passed out. I have a journal of Sarah's from that time. She vacillated between being madly in love with her "soul mate" Tyson and wondering if he was cheating on her. She hated her body, described it as fat and disgusting, documenting her use of diet pills and throwing up after meals. She wrote about being an addict.

> I am addicted to a drug and it has been haunting me all day. I want to do some so bad but I can't. I really wish I could, my body hurts so much. I hate it.
>
> —Sarah's journal, February 14, 2007

Sarah and Tyson moved from oxy to heroin, which was much cheaper. I would find small squares of tinfoil in jackets she had borrowed, could see a glint of silver flashing from her purse as she rummaged for a cigarette. She smelled like vinegar or chocolate that had turned bad. I knew something had shifted in her, that she had moved past partying and into something stickier that I couldn't quite understand. No one else in my life was doing these kinds of drugs. Outside of cocaine, I had no knowledge of the world she was living in. She didn't want to talk about it. The only thing I could think to do was yell at her. It didn't help.

Sarah and Tyson broke up after a series of blowout fights and cheating accusations. Sarah quickly moved on to Blake, which was not his real name but the name he sometimes went by. He drove his car too fast and regularly got tickets for throwing lit cigarettes from a moving vehicle.

. . .

The day I told her she could have any life she wanted, Sharon and I had driven to the apartment where Sarah and Blake lived to convince Sarah to go to rehab. Since they had started dating, I could not recall seeing my sister without pinpoint pupils and droopy eyelids. The two of them were noticeably high when we arrived. Blake couldn't control the volume of his voice, shout-asking us if we wanted anything to drink. It was a little surreal, Sarah telling us she hadn't used in days before nodding off on the couch while Blake bellowed that the two of them could get clean at home. I finally got Sarah up and convinced her to go out to my truck.

"Take this." I handed her the chip. "And when you hit thirty days, I want you to give me yours."

She went to North River Rehab a few days later, a facility within reasonable driving distance from us. Sarah would manage to do quite a bit in those thirty days, but getting clean wasn't one of them.

Liar Gene

My father smelled like cigarettes and trees. He wrote a book that was published in French, a language he didn't speak. He never paid child support. He was dear friends with gay rights activists Harry Hay and John Burnside. He spent a third of his life training to be a medicine man with a Yurok Indian doctor. He was a liar. Sometimes I was a liar too.

My father grew up on a dude ranch in Tucson, Arizona. His parents were first cousins who married to piss off his mother's holy-rolling preacher father. After they eloped, they ran away and joined a vaudeville troupe and eventually worked the rodeo circuit. My grandfather breathed fire and participated in lasso competitions. My grandmother was a trick rider. I have a picture of her dangling dangerously off her horse: her arms are outstretched, and there is a wide, full smile on her face. I think she was already pregnant with my father when that picture was taken.

My father had an older brother named Rex. When Gary was two years old and Rex was four, their mom split and left the two boys behind. My father grew up in the company of cowboys, horses, and the desert. His days were long, and the chores brutal. I grew up hearing stories about the violence cowboys inflicted on their own bodies, cattle that somehow got stuck in the tops of trees, and days when Gary would point his horse in any direction and wander off into the desert. He told me a story once of a young boy on a nearby ranch who was accidentally hanged to death during a game of cops and robbers. "It's hard to hang a man," he'd say. "I wasn't playing with them that day, but I sure as hell coulda been." His childhood sounded like an old movie.

My father told me that my grandfather was a prostitute. Rich men would send their wives and children to the dude ranch for the authentic cowboy experience, and my grandfather would take the wives on night rides that ended with sweaty saddle blankets and large tips. He eventually remarried, to a woman both brothers described as a monster. My father didn't speak of her often, but I heard of cigarette burns, little hands held over hot stoves, and bathroom doors kept open in order to humiliate. When Rex turned sixteen, he ran away. Two years later my father followed.

Gary cheated, a lot. My mother, in turn, was mad, a lot. Furious, she once took a giant container of cinnamon and shook it all over the seats of his Toyota. For months, he smelled like the angriest I had ever seen her. He was legally married twice, but never to her. They had a wedding; I was there. I was six years old, and my sister was an infant. In every picture I have my hand up my dress, scratching and pulling at the itchy tights I had to wear. But after their ceremony, my father refused to sign the marriage license.

These are a few small details about my father's life—the ones I believe are most true. I have spent a portion of my adult life turning over these and other stories about my father and examining them, looking for a pattern to the truths and the lies. I have searched for the thread that connects him to me, to the behaviors in me that signal I am his daughter. I was a good liar. I have an ability to adapt to different groups of people to fit in. I can be charming. Strangers like to tell me secrets. I have used all these to my advantage. I have been ashamed of doing so, but I have still done it.

. . .

My sister started lying very young. Small things at first, denying she had made a mess or pretending she hadn't borrowed something. My father punished us when we lied to him but encouraged lying to others, especially when it came to our mother. "Deny, deny, deny," he always told us.

When Sarah was eleven, she told us her choir group was doing a medley of songs from *Moulin Rouge*, and she had been chosen as lead soloist. For months, we helped her rehearse. She would stand in Sharon's living room and belt out: "*One day I'll fly away, leave all this to yesterday.*" We followed along with sheet music, making sure she got the lyrics right and running lines from some of the patter. She told us about practicing choreography and had my mom drop her off for costume fittings. The whole family knew every song by heart. My mother eventually ran into Sarah's choir leader at the local co-op. "We are all so excited to see the big performance," my mom told her.

The choir director looked puzzled. "You mean the one coming up in spring?"

"No, the *Moulin Rouge* medley. Sarah told us all about it."

"I'm sorry," the choir director replied. "I have no idea what you're talking about."

In a phone call to a family friend, Kim, an incredulous Sharon relayed the story. Kim was silent for a moment. "This is really serious," she said. "She could be a pathological liar."

> *In less than three months I should be graduating high school but I am not. Instead I am laying in this bed. I will wake up tomorrow around two, eat some food, shower and then go on my daily hustle to find some way of making money so I can buy drugs.*
>
> —Sarah's journal, April 5, 2007

. . .

When I was a young teenager, I was obsessed with pigs. I swore off all bacon and pork chops and even briefly adopted a pet pig that lived nearby on a farm. On a warm summer day, my stepmom made a big stack of bacon for BLT sandwiches for her and my father. I was sitting in the kitchen, reading a book, while the bacon sat resting on the counter. The smell was irresistible, so I snuck a piece, and then another and then another, until only a few pieces were left. When my stepmom came back inside to make sandwiches, she searched for the bacon thief, and I pointed the finger at my sister. Though she was only seven years old at the time, my sister's habit of lying was well-known, and she loved bacon. It was an easy sell, despite her protests that she had done nothing.

For years, the story of the stolen bacon was told in my family. It so nicely illustrated my sister's sneaky personality, her willingness to lie in the face of irrefutable proof. The story evolved: eventually my stepmom even claimed to have seen bacon grease smeared on Sarah's mouth. I occasionally brought up the missing bacon story because I didn't want anyone to forget it. Many years later, when my sister was nearing nineteen, even she began to believe the myth, and confessed to having eaten the bacon. My sister's own memory of the incident had changed: she believed my lie.

I kept it going for a few more years after that before I admitted to everyone that I was the one who had eaten the bacon. We were sitting in my stepmom's remote mountain home, she and I reading while Sarah paced the room, trying to find cell reception. I looked up from my book and said casually, "Hey, remember the bacon? I was the one who ate it." My sister shrieked, and Sharon dissolved into laughter.

"I always get blamed for everything," Sarah protested.

"I know," I said, grinning. "That's why it was a perfect long con."

She looked at me.

"I can't believe you kept this up for so long."

"It just got funnier every year," I replied. Then we laughed.

. . .

My worst lies happened when I was drinking and using coke. Stealing—probably $10,000—from my mother, writing checks to myself, swiping her debit card. I took beer from the sandwich shop I worked at and did lines on their yellowing toilet seat. I fucked married men and sad men and scary men. I categorized my lying: social lies, omissions, white lies, gray lies, kind lies, terrible lies. I am the one friends call when they need a perfect lie for missing work. I have lied in most of my relationships and never been caught. Through the process of sobriety, I have tried to address this part of my past personality. I apologize when I am in the wrong. I make amends quickly. Instead of lying, I curate my life story so that I can hide the most vulnerable parts. I will still lie about certain things: my depression, the feeling of relief when I vomit after overeating, anxiety about money.

I don't know why I never questioned my father's insistence that we lie to our mother, that we keep things from her. Do we inherit such behaviors? I wake up most days with a monster curled up in my chest, softly growling. I have to take a few moments before I swing my legs over the side of the bed to remind myself that I need to be a good person today. I am convinced I am no good. My sister, too, was convinced she was no good.

Perhaps this was because we knew, on some level, that our father was not a good man. Or that he was not a good man when he lied and cheated and stole. He was the best storyteller I've ever heard, he could play guitar beautifully, and when he focused his attention on you, it felt like the most brilliant, warm light. How do you reconcile the monster and the man? At the end of his life, my father was not speaking to any of his children. He was in a long-distance relationship with a woman in the Philippines who he "married" and then sent money to every week. He lived off-grid in a one-bedroom cabin he built. After he died, pictures of all his children were found framed on every wall of his house. This is what I am afraid I will become.

During the one-year period my sister was sober, she made amends to me as part of her twelve-step program. She apologized for stealing from me: money, drugs, clothing. She told me she used to cut the cocaine I would buy from her because she liked the idea that she was fucking me over. She said she was sorry for all the times she faked a crisis so she could get money, sympathy, or a ride. I had made my amends to her a few years prior. I cannot remember what I apologized for.

I make amends to her now, sitting on the back porch of our mountain home. I say, I am sorry we had the father we did. I am sorry that he tried to put inside us the worst parts of himself. I wish that I had told you more often that I didn't just love you, I liked you. I am sorry that I so often reduced you to your addiction, to your lies. I regret not hugging you the last time I saw you. I am sorry. I am so sorry that I am here and you are not.

I am a weak human being who is bitching about her life but is too weak to even change it. So I will stop bitching and face reality. This is who I am, and I hate every inch of my pathetic, ugly, weak self.

—Sarah's journal, April 5, 2007

Coming Home

I graduated from Sarah Lawrence with my BA in 2009, when I was twenty-six years old, during one of the coldest winters I had ever experienced in New York. After my post-high-school cancer diagnosis, a year living in Italy, and time taken off to address my own mental health and sobriety, it had been a long road to my diploma.

The day I flew home, just a week before Christmas, I called my family over and over again, but no one would answer their phone. Sitting on the floor of the San Francisco airport, waiting for the last leg of my trip to board, I finally reached my mother.

"I have to tell you something." She sounded exhausted.

"Is she dead?" I asked, trying to keep my voice calm.

"No." She paused. "Brian woke up early this morning, and Sarah wasn't breathing." Brian was Sarah's current boyfriend; he was a friend of Jed's, and I was pretty sure he was far too nice to stay her boyfriend for long. "She was cold, and her skin looked blue." My mom's voice shook. "Jed came in and did CPR." Our brother had been an EMT at one point. "The paramedics said that if he hadn't, she would have died." I hardly spoke, just nodded along while she told me about the ambulance, the hospital, Sarah's condition. I boarded my last flight terrified and resentful; instead of celebrating my graduation, I was heading home to convince Sarah she again needed to go to rehab.

. . .

I visited her at the hospital the day after my flight home. She looked thin and pale. Her voice was hoarse when we spoke. I laid my hand on her cool forehead and asked her what happened.

"You know what happened," she said, a little sullen, and I pulled my hand away.

"I know you almost died," I replied. "But I don't understand what happened."

Sarah snorted derisively. "I'm an addict—isn't that what you've been telling Jed for months?" This was true; I had been trying to convince Jed of her drug use for a while, but he was insistent that she was clean, that she wouldn't lie to him.

I tried to ignore her tone. "Are you okay?" I asked.

"What do you think?"

I didn't respond. The silence stretched awkwardly between us.

"I mean, I'm not great." Her voice cracked.

"What do you want to do now?"

"Honestly?" She sighed. "I want to get high."

"Will you go back to rehab?"

"Fuuuck." Sarah laid her head back on the hospital pillow, tears forming at the corners of her eyes. "I guess I don't have a choice."

"You have a choice."

She looked at me. "You know that's not true."

We sat staring at the beige walls of St. Joseph's Hospital, light filtering through the slatted blinds that covered the small windows. "Okay, I'll do it." She sounded resigned.

"Okay, I'll start looking for a place." I got up to leave.

"Rose?"

"Yeah?"

"I was wearing Santa lingerie."

"What?"

"When the ambulance came, I was in Santa lingerie."

And we both laughed.

. . .

More details unfolded over the next few days: Jed's children, Mena and Maggie, had been home when Sarah overdosed; Brian suspected she had been using for a while; Sarah had been high around the kids, possibly while she babysat them. I was tasked with finding an affordable rehab that Sarah would agree to. I sat her down and told her she had to check in within ninety days, or I couldn't be in her life anymore. She reluctantly agreed.

Black Box

My mother paid for Sarah's first rehab, the one she attended in 2009, while using with Blake. North River Rehab cost $8,000 for thirty days, but I don't think any of us were happy with the level of supervision or care provided. Sarah was able to:

Hide drugs in her bags, so she didn't detox for the first few days.

Sneak a cell phone in, so she could call Blake.

Hook up with a guy in the program.

Convince her group therapy that she started using because my mother kicked her out of the car in Oakland, leaving her homeless.

Convince all the other attendees that she was a DJ named Scratch.

It was lax. The next one would be much stricter. Neither took.

The day her treatment ended at North River, my mom, Sharon, and I stood in the parking lot and watched as she got into Blake's car. They sped off, leaving us covered in dust. Sarah later told me she got high on the drive home. Somewhere between the first rehab and the second, she started shooting up in addition to smoking.

. . .

An addict has to be ready to get clean, want to do the work of sobriety, want to feel again. Having been an addict myself, I'm not sure why it was so hard for me to see this. I really thought I could want it for her. Or that I could *be* that part for her. I was ready to get sober, Sarah should also be ready. Both times Sarah went to rehab, it was because I told her she had to or she would die or lose her family. I didn't take into consideration that she didn't want to get clean.

We couldn't afford to send Sarah to a "good" rehab center, a place that was properly staffed, with comprehensive and holistic treatment, including licensed therapists and psychiatrists. Looking at facilities for Sarah, I found that the presence of even one licensed therapist meant a cost of $20,000 a month on the lower end, and upwards of $60,000 a month for the more fully staffed, pricier centers.

I've since learned that addiction treatment represents a $35 billion industry in the United States. There are more than 14,500 centers that specialize in substance abuse, but there are no federal standards regulating the industry. As a result, there is very little oversight for recovery facilities in the United States. There is even less oversight for halfway houses and sober-living homes. Investigative reporters have unearthed terrible stories about rehab systems in California, Florida, and New York, just to name a few—profitable empires of transitional housing, with no scientific support, that are pervaded by fraud.* Rarely is the rehab industry accountable for a standard of evidence-based care for addicts, and rarely does it practice evidence-based care, such as cross-treating drug addiction and mental health issues, which, I can see now, Sarah needed.

. . .

I chose Sarah's second rehab, Shining Light Recovery, for two reasons: it was far away from Sarah's addict friends so they couldn't come see her, and it cost only $3,000 a month with a payment plan option. Within a couple weeks, though, she was kicked out for showering with another girl. Sexual conduct was not allowed, so she moved to a women's sober-living house.

Living at that house led to Sarah's longest stretch of sobriety since she started using, about a year. It was one of the first times in her life she lived with only women.

---

* See especially: Kim Barker's reporting for the *New York Times* on "Three-Quarter" homes; Cat Ferguson's reporting for *BuzzFeed* on South Florida's Delray Beach; and Hillel Aron's reporting for *LA Weekly* on Los Angeles's "Rehab Mogul"

She had to do chores, cook, attend meetings, be account-able to her roommates, and get a sponsor. It gave her a foundation of skills to build on. In some ways, Sarah was forever fifteen. She had difficulty making dinner or handling a bank account or setting a schedule for herself. While other people her age were learning how to do laundry or write a check, Sarah was in a bus with her band of lost boys, festival hopping and dropping Molly. While her high school classmates applied to college, started jobs, or took gap years to travel, Sarah was ransacking unlocked cars for wallets, iPhones, and cameras she could pawn.

She had a different set of skills that weren't entirely useful as she tried to reenter the world newly clean and sober. Her first instinct was to hustle. When do our instincts take root? I think often about the timing of our different entry points—into substance abuse and recovery. By the time I entered sobriety, years after my turn to dark drinking, I had already lived on my own, navigated cancer and the subsequent treatment. I had developed a basic skill set for dealing with the logistics of adulthood. When I got sober, I had something to return to, a knowledge base that provided me with a little structure. When Sarah got clean, it was like she was trying to learn to walk before she could even crawl.

About six months into sobriety, she signed up for community college courses. My mother and Sharon urged her to take just one or two classes, get a feel for the work-load, so she wouldn't be overwhelmed. Instead, she took a full load of units. She dropped most of the classes before the semester was over. She felt like she would never catch up to her peers. The sense of insurmountability made it difficult for her to move past perceived failures; if she couldn't make it through one full semester, how could she ever be successful academically?

> *I hate who I am. I hate the person that drugs make me into. It is not me anymore breathing my breath—it is all the drugs—talking, laughing, crying through my life. You might as well suck the coating off me, chop me up and snort me.*
>
> *—Sarah's journal, April 5, 2007*

SMALL TOWN, USA—On Sunday, Oct. 20, at 7:05 P.M., the female victim of a shooting on Friday night at Little Tree Trailer Park succumbed to her injuries and died. The male victim had been pronounced dead on the scene late Friday night.

The victims have now been identified as Clayton Sparks, 32, and Lindsey Levy, 29. Next of kin have been notified.

Sheriff's officials released a statement saying that the case was being investigated as a robbery and double homicide. They do not believe the victims were involved in the burglary, saying, "From what we can tell, Clayton Sparks interrupted a robbery in progress and was shot during a subsequent altercation."

Investigators were hopeful that Lindsey Levy would recover and be able to provide a statement about what happened, but unfortunately Levy never regained consciousness.

The owner of the trailer that had been burgled has been notified and returned early Sunday to assess the damage. Edgar Duran reported to police that cash, jewelry, and an antique watch were missing. There was also significant damage to the trailer as well as to a safe belonging to Duran that was blasted open, most likely with the same gun used in the murders.

Small Town, USA

S mall Town is a specific city and every city. It has high incidences of violence, sexual assaults, and drug overdoses. It is dangerous for women. It is also a place where people live and work and make babies and wake up every day.

News articles talk about the rate of violent crimes soaring in Small Town. People go there to vacation. It has parks and tourist attractions, recreation sites and restaurants. Locals complain about rampant drug use, mainly opioids and meth. There is little infrastructure set up to deal with the crisis.

. . .

Small Town is where Sarah dated two boys at once, a fraught love triangle that would last for several years. It is where Sarah drove a large black truck while drinking Red Bull and blasting hip-hop. It is the site of Sarah's second try at getting clean. Small Town is where my mother flew to tell my sister that our dad was in a coma. It is where Sarah worked as a pizza delivery driver, a barista, an office assistant, and a drug dealer. It is where Sarah died. Small Town is where I drove her one May day to Olive Garden for unlimited breadsticks and then dropped her off at Shining Light rehab. I have regretted it ever since.

I visited her there just once, for a sobriety conference. I have pictures of Sarah and me from that trip. The sky is pink behind us, and our cheeks are pressed together. We are smiling.

Ghoul

The last time I talked to my father, he told me I was a ghoul. I was sitting in my college dorm room, junior year, as he yelled at me over the phone. "You are a ghoul," he shouted. "You're a liar, a fucking thief."

"Gary, Gary, Gary." I tried to say his name to break the relentless screaming. I repeated it like a mantra, hoping it would block out what he was saying. He eventually heard me.

"You don't know me well enough to call me by my name," he spat.

"Actually, I don't know you well enough to call you Dad," I replied in a shaky voice.

"You greedy fucking ghoul of a daughter," he shouted back. "You don't deserve one fucking ounce of good from this life. You ghoul."

He said this, over and over and over, until his voice became hoarse. I hung up. My ears were ringing. My dictionary was sitting on my desk, I felt like I could still hear him shouting. I flipped to the word *ghoul*: "an evil spirit or phantom, especially one supposed to rob graves and feed on dead bodies." The sample sentence: "A wicked ghoul was suspected of all the terrible crimes committed in the town."

All the terrible crimes.

. . .

When I picked up the phone to speak to him, two years after our estrangement, the conversation started off politely enough. He did not behave as if we had spent the last two years not talking. He told me he had heard I was writing and asked how I was. I brought up the reason for my call, mainly that he had been harassing my mother with incessant calls about money he thought she owed him. "Fucking ghoul," he roared at me as soon as I said this.

I took the things he said about me and carefully tucked them inside my body. The word *ghoul* floats through my bloodstream even now; I carry it with me.

The last time he spoke to my sister was over email. They were arguing over money. He told her that she was the biggest disappointment of his life, and he hoped she fell asleep with a needle in her arm.

. . .

When my father was fifty-nine years old, a few years after everyone in my family had stopped speaking to him, he had a stroke and fell down and hit his head. A friend tried to take him to a doctor, but he refused to go. Shortly thereafter, he had another stroke and had to go to the hospital.

A week later, my mom received a phone call from one of my father's friends, looking for my sister and me, as we were Gary's next of kin. The hospital needed us to make decisions regarding his care. By the time we were contacted, he was in a coma. He could not see or hear us. He could not even call me a terrible name I could stitch onto my skin. He was just a body that could not breathe on its own anymore.

I had no illusions that I would repair my relationship with my father. I never imagined some long-time-coming reconciliation. But I thought of him often. I dreamed of cowboys, wild horses, and rattlesnakes. I wrote stories for fiction class about men who could breathe fire, little boys hung by accident in a dude-ranch barn, cows stuck in desert trees.

Sarah was in rehab at Shining Light. She'd been there for about a week when my mother flew over to tell her in person. I worried that the news, coming so soon into an in-patient program, might trigger her to use. I also knew it might trigger a desire for recovery.

Shining Light allowed her to leave so she could see him. My entire family—my mom, sister, and brother—went to be with him, stayed overnight, and took turns holding his hand. I went, but only for a minute, after Sarah came out to my truck, parked in the hospital lot, and told me I would regret not saying goodbye. "He is waiting for you before he lets go," she said to me, and took my hand, pulling me toward the hospital doors.

I hovered in the doorway of his room and heard him breathe a terrible, rattling breath. I watched his face, his beautiful wrinkles, struggle against the machines keeping him alive. His hair was grayer than I remembered. I wanted to go over and smell him, to see if the father I knew when I was young would materialize in a haze of smoke and pine. I looked at my sister, who had taken a seat, her hand

Sober

in his, whispering quietly in his direction. She looked so young.

In that moment, I wished to be a ghoul. I ached to float over to my father and press my lips against his gaping gray mouth. I wanted to suck the death out of him. I imagined all his terrible crimes leaving his body in one violent exhalation and entering mine. Maybe that is what he was screaming at me all those years ago: what he saw in himself. *You are a ghoul. You're a liar, a fucking thief.* Maybe he was asking me to take it all away, all those monstrous feelings. For all his storytelling, he could never tell the truth. He could never say *I need help to be a better person.* He thought if he yelled loudly enough that I would understand, that I would save him at the very end. I would rob his grave, feed on his body, and absolve him. I'd like to think that he wanted the best of himself left for that moment, for my sister, who insisted on holding the hand of the man who had called her the biggest disappointment of his life.

. . .

She returned from his deathbed to Shining Light Recovery. She would stay sober for one year after his death.

Drug of Choice

My drug of choice was alcohol or cocaine, but preferably both at the same time. Sarah's drug of choice was heroin or boys. Preferably guys who would make her feel loved and wanted and chosen, and if they liked to slam dope, all the better.

After our father's death, Sarah went back to rehab, only to be promptly kicked out for violating the no-sexual-contact rule. She moved into a sober-living house in the same small town and committed to staying there for at least thirty days while attending meetings regularly. It is advised (although not explicitly written in any of the AA or NA literature) that people who are not already in a relationship refrain from dating and sex for the first year of sobriety. Sex and alcohol were inextricably linked for me, so I chose to stay single for two years after my first AA meeting. It forced me to focus on the blood and guts of my dysfunction, without any distractions. In the end, my hiatus didn't stop me from dating assholes.

Sarah met Cory and then Mike and then Don and then Ryan, who was Cory's best friend. She met Ryan at an AA meeting. He was on probation for drug-related charges. Within six months he would be in prison for failing a drug test and violating his parole. He wouldn't get out for a year. Sarah left her sober-living house and moved into his family's home. He and Sarah stayed together. They fought. They got engaged. She cheated on him; he broke up with her. They wrote long letters to each other. They got back together. She bought her own engagement ring and drove his giant black truck to her job delivering pizzas for Papa John's.

Sarah was sober, Sarah was slipping, Sarah met Jack and stopped writing to Ryan, except sometimes. A sometimes-sober Sarah dated both Jack and Ryan, floating between the two depending on whom she was fighting with or loving too hard. She fell off the wagon and took some pills, then got back on and started spending time with her new sponsor. Sarah introduced oxy to Jack, who liked to drink, and they drove around in his big truck drinking beer, sometimes getting high. Ryan came back from prison, and Jack became the side piece who occasionally was the main piece, depending on the day of the week. She would steal from these boys: money, credit cards, a shotgun once. They always forgave her. The stolen items were rarely returned.

Sarah and I fought over text about Ryan, Jack, and oxy. We sent misspelled, angrily typed messages criticizing each other's life choices. She drove to Humboldt to visit and would spend the entire time with her friends or on the phone with one of the boys who loved her.

I remember standing over Sarah one day while she was on Facebook, about a year before her death, and seeing a photo on her timeline. "Who the fuck is that?" I said, pointing at a man in the picture who had *14/88* tattooed on his forearm. I knew the hate those numbers represented. "And why the fuck are you friends with him?" They had met in recovery, she explained, and she felt sorry for him because his appearance alienated him from most people. They had become so close, they referred to each other as brother and sister.

"He looks like a Nazi. Why would you hang out with someone who is a white supremacist?" I asked her angrily. She tried telling me that he had only gotten the tattoo because he joined a white power group while in prison, for protection. We got into an argument. She told me I needed to believe that people could change, that, being in AA, I should practice forgiveness and understanding and that I was being judgmental. I told her she was an idiot and naive. We didn't talk about him again.

I cried into my One Line a Day journal. For a whole year, every entry is about either how much I am worried about Sarah—fragmented, messy sentences that read "Wtf, Sarah" or "I am afraid one day she won't call anymore"—or

Swimming with her friend Noelle

complaining about my weight. I watched her life on Facebook, her long blond hair windswept as she took pictures while driving, a can of sugar-free Red Bull in her hand. She was beautiful, and I was tired.

Sarah lied about being sober and then told the truth and then got sober again. She moved back to Salmon Creek, the area where our stepmom lived, to work and get away from bad habits. She moved into a tiny cabin with her childhood best friend, Tess, and they worked outdoors in the heat and swam in the river in the afternoons. Sarah called her sponsor, Lynn, every day and worked hard to save up for a trip to Thailand she wanted to take.

But the boys, the boys, the boys remained. Sometimes not Jack or Ryan but mostly them. She couldn't quit for any significant period of time. The heroin yes, but the boys no. Or maybe they were connected. The drugs and the boys always came back together. There was no way to separate them. I begged her to go to therapy to talk about the boys, the drugs, anything. She looked at me and said, "I can't go to therapy, they will want me to talk about Dad." And I realized then that the grief of losing our father, long before he was ever dead, had so wounded my sister that she didn't know where to begin.

PART III

The Gun

A Fable

The Tattooed Criminal and the Liability decide one night to rob a home. This home, a trailer, sits in a mostly vacant RV park on the edges of their small town. They drive to this property late at night because they know there are drugs, money, and valuables there. They believe the inhabitants of the trailer are gone, out of town for a few days. They take a gun, an old shotgun sold to them by a friend who stole it from her boyfriend. They say the shotgun is just for show, to scare anyone in case they are interrupted during their crime.

They break into the trailer easily; the Tattooed Criminal has been there several times and knows its weak spots. The Liability is directed to look through the closets and small dresser for cash and valuables while the Tattooed Criminal works on the safe he has seen the owner of the trailer place things in: drugs and an old watch that he believes is worth a great deal. He thinks he has figured out the code, observing this dealer the few times he has come here to buy from him.

Ten minutes pass, the Liability has filled his pockets with jewelry, money, and a Pez dispenser he thinks his kid will like. The Tattooed Criminal has not been as lucky; he has been unable to open the safe. He kicks and punches and swears but it will not open for him. In a rage, he picks up the shotgun he has brought and blasts off two shots at the unyielding lock. The two men laugh when it opens for them. They do not think of the noise.

The gunshots wake up a Sleeping Man in a neighboring trailer. He tells his Sleeping Girlfriend to wait in bed, he will investigate. He encounters the two men as they are leaving the trailer, their stolen goods and reloaded gun in hand. The Tattooed Criminal threatens the Sleeping Man, tells him to go back to his home and forget he ever saw them. To prove his point, he uses the shotgun to try and push the man down. It goes off, suddenly and loudly, killing him. The Sleeping Man is now a Dead Man.

The Sleeping Girlfriend is awake. She has pressed her face to the window, and she watches as her boyfriend's body collapses. Maybe she screamed. The Tattooed Criminal and the Liability look up and see her face, distorted in horror. They decide that she should die too. She has seen them, knows their faces, their tattoos, the sounds of their voices. One more shot rings in the RV park, the Sleeping Lovers bleed, and the two men leave.

. . .

The stolen property is divided up between the robbers, some of it sold. There is tension between them. The Tattooed Criminal does not trust the Liability. Just look at his name.

Another person enters this story now. He is, simply, the Man.

The Man has helped sell some of the stolen goods and drugs. He receives a cut of the profits for his part in the crime. He is an old friend of the Tattooed Criminal and whispers in his ear, warns him that the Liability will rat him out to the police. They are all high, and soon, the Tattooed Criminal is hearing whispers even when the Man is not in the room.

It is clear the Man does not like the Liability. Perhaps he believes that he should have been there the night of the robbery-gone-wrong instead of the Liability. Perhaps he simply wants a larger cut. Late one night, the Man and the Liability get into an argument in the Tattooed Criminal's house. There is a knife. There is a beating. The Tattooed Criminal enters the scene at some point, sees the Liability, maybe dying or suffering or living, we do not know. He takes the knife from the Man and finishes the job.

They do not know how to dispose of a whole body. It's too much for them. The Tattooed Criminal and the Man take the Liability into the garage, where there are tools and sharp things. The whole becomes parts and these make more sense to them. They drive and scatter, like they are feeding the reaper's birds.

Three people dead. One shotgun sold by a girl, by my sister. Fifteen days after the first part of the Liability is found, she too will be dead.

The Dog

When the Man comes to the door, the dog lets out a low growl and stands in front of her, guarding her small body. The dog doesn't like the Man; he smells sick, like burnt sugar. She puts her hand on the dog's head to quiet him, so he swallows the snarl held in his throat. She always knows best. She also smells like burnt sugar, but there are other smells on her too: wet trees, smoke, lemon. She lets the Man in, they hug, and she laughs, briefly.

She and the Man leave. The dog can hear his car engine rev as he pulls away from the house. While they are gone, the dog drinks and drinks from the bowl of cool water left for him on the kitchen tile. The dog gets unreasonably thirsty after seeing the Man. He sniffs around her piles of clothes until he finds his favorite sweatshirt. He turns two and a half times before settling into the warm smell of her, and falls asleep.

He is surprised awake when they return. He jumps up and begins to bark after she has opened the front door to come back inside. The Man is laughing as she leads him to the kitchen. The Man is not afraid of the dog in the slightest. The dog is ashamed, imagines his teeth piercing his fleshy calf. The dog decides to stay in the living room and chew on his own front paw. She would yell at him if he bit the Man. He chews and bites until flecks of blood appear, his feathery white fur turning to wet rust.

He hears the two of them go into the bathroom. He stiffens, anticipating the door closing, but it doesn't. He relaxes—she is still within reach. He could still go to her and put his head against her body until she rubs the tips of his ears.

But he waits, he listens. She does not like it when he goes to her while she and the Man are in the bathroom. Soon the Man will leave and she will come to the couch, tilt her head back, and fall into a place that is neither sleep nor wakefulness. The dog will lie down, push her body into the crevice of the couch so he can stretch out beside her. He will put his wet nose on her chin to check her waning breath. This is what happens after her trips to the bathroom. He knows this.

The dog grows bored waiting for the Man to leave. He looks out the sliding glass doors at the stretch of field behind the house. Just beyond the field are woods, full of moss, birds, and endless miles to run. He likes to run. Sometimes, even though he loves her, he leaves. He runs despite her shouts and pleas for him to return. He runs until he cannot hear her voice or anything but the flapping of his ears in the forest air. He runs away from days spent on the couch, her waning breath, this Man, all the men.

There is a noise from the bathroom: a strangled cough followed by a wet gurgle. The dog runs from the glass doors toward her just as the Man exits the bathroom. The dog catches only a glimpse of her: she is sitting on the bathroom floor, her hand weakly outstretched, the gurgling noise coming from her throat and lungs. He can smell vomit and blood. She is looking right at him. He holds her gaze, running to her, but the Man closes the door too quickly. The dog snarls at him, bares his teeth, and lunges. The Man kicks the dog away, swearing, then darts to the front door.

The dog turns his attention to the bathroom. He can hear her, hear the sounds her body is making, the waning of her breath apparent to him even though his wet nose is not pressed to her chin. He howls, using his paws to claw and tear at the door separating them. He barks, frustrated that he is not strong enough to break through the wood and get to her. He hears her body slide and hit the door. He becomes quiet, pressing his belly to the floor and pushing his nose to the crack between the door and the tile. He whines into the crack, begging her to make a noise. He stays there, willing his breath to travel to her mouth and make her alive. He lies there until he falls asleep.

. . .

The smell is unmistakable when he awakens. Still, he calls out to her. He is desperately thirsty and drinks from his water bowl until there is nothing left. He shits in the corner of the room, far away from the smell of the bathroom and the pile of her clothes. He eats and eats and then returns to the crack in the door.

. . .

There is no more water or food. He has been unable to tear down the door, so he has ripped up the couch, peed on the carpet, pressed his paws to the glass doors leading to the field, and cried out. He has turned over the trash can, sniffing through the garbage to find anything to eat. At one point, he heard the mailman come to the door and knock—he barked and barked, but the mailman left. The dog's throat is sore, his paws are tender, his stomach aches. With his teeth, he pulls her sweatshirt gingerly from the pile of her clothes over to the door. He buries his head in the smell of wet trees, smoke, and lemon.

. . .

The boy comes home. The dog runs around the house, howling her name and crying for help. The boy opens the bathroom door, and despite trying to get to her body for the last four days, the dog turns away from the sight of her.

Promises to the Universe

I dreamed once that my sister was having a baby. She gave birth in a small, strange room with the whole family watching. The doctor informed us all that a second baby was coming, and no one was more surprised than my sister. Sarah delivered her second baby, but no one bothered to catch it, so it lay in the middle of the delivery room floor and cried. My sister picked up the first baby and went to leave the room. When she got to the door, she turned back to us and said, with a small shrug, "I only wanted the one," and left.

I dreamed once that I had a baby and then ate it.

. . .

Sarah's time in Salmon Creek, near Sharon's house, started out hopeful. Then Sarah became secretive. The computer at Sharon's was hardly ever used because the only internet available was dial-up. I needed to find a recipe, so I braved the slow connection. When I went to the browser's search engine, the last few searches popped up: *how to stop a miscarriage?* I looked over at my sister, sitting on the couch. She was twenty-three years old, and after a year of sobriety had been slipping in and out of the program. I was pretty sure she was using again: she was painfully thin, always complaining of being tired, her pupils perpetually tiny.

"Sarah," I said. "Can we talk outside?" She gave me a dubious look but followed me out to the front porch.

"What's up?" she asked.

"I don't know how to ask this, but I was using the computer and saw a search about miscarriages." I trailed off, my voice as gentle as I could make it. She looked at me and sighed, pulled a pack of cigarettes out of her back pocket, and lit one using the box of matches balanced on a planter box.

"Yeah." She paused, her eyes and mouth momentarily squeezed tight. "It happened last week, that's why I was sick." She took a drag from her cigarette and looked out over the cold afternoon. I watched her breath and smoke hit the chilly air and drift away from us.

"You wanted to keep it?" I asked.

"Yeah, I did."

I raised my eyebrows at her. This was not the first time we'd had a conversation about her being pregnant, but it was the first time she had answered yes to that question.

"Was Ryan the father?"

"I think so." She sounded reluctant. "I mean, that's why Ryan's parents came to visit." I nodded—she had seen them recently.

"They must have been excited."

"Actually, we all got in a big fight."

"Why?"

She took another long drag and laughed bitterly. "Because they thought the baby was Jack's and were upset about it. Ryan defended me, though. Everyone was yelling."

"Could it have been Jack's?" I asked.

Sarah shrugged and put her cigarette out, balancing the butt precariously in the overflowing abalone shell she used as an ashtray.

"Does it matter?"

I didn't know how to respond, so I simply asked, "Are you okay?" She looked surprised when I asked this. Which was fair. I didn't have the best history of being kind instead of critical when it came to some of her life choices. I'm sure she was expecting a lecture.

"I dunno." For a second, I thought she was about to cry.

"Can I ask what made you want to keep it this time?"

"Well, I love Ryan, and it would be hard to go through an abortion again . . ." She trailed off, shook her head, and then grimaced. "I thought maybe it would make things different."

"What things?"
"My life."

. . .

My sister had six abortions. Or four. Or eight. It depends on who you ask and what you believe. I do know that on multiple occasions her young body went to the clinic so she could end a pregnancy. The nurses told her that if she continued to have evacuations, she could scar her uterus and be unable to have kids later on. "When you're ready," they said. I would tease her that she was so fertile, she could get knocked up just by someone looking at her.

I can't have children. One of the chemotherapy drugs I was on damaged my ovaries. This, coupled with my endometriosis, has all but ensured kids aren't in my future. I have never wanted to be a mother, never thought I would be a good one. After all, I could eat my baby or watch her drown or let her die at the hands of monsters.

But I watched Sarah take pregnancy test after pregnancy test, and I quietly seethed. I picked up phone calls to listen to her cry about another abortion and hid my fury. She is using up all our baby chances, I thought. There won't be any left for me. I knew it was irrational. I did not want my own children, but I resented that Sarah had the option. I wanted her to stop getting pregnant. I wanted her to stop doing something so fucking well that I could not do at all. When I imagined my sister, belly round and glowing, I became enraged.

. . .

The only time I wanted a child was in the first few months after Sarah's death. I was having nightly panic attacks, thinking of her body on the bathroom floor, wondering what her last thoughts were. As my partner slept beside me, I would sit in the dark, willing myself to breathe. I'd imagine holding a baby until I could feel my heart rate slow and the panic subside. At the time, I thought that these were the first signs of wanting a baby, that perhaps it had just come to me later than most. Sarah could no longer have one, I would have to do it.

I watched my pregnant friend's belly. "It's like an alien," I shrieked, and Andrea laughed, lovingly running her hands over her squirming son. She described to me the different ways he moved inside her, how his feet pressed against her rib cage. I asked her a million questions. Despite her best efforts, I felt no closer to understanding what it was to have a body inside your own. I put my hand on her stomach and marveled: what a strange, remarkable thing it is to create a person.

It is tempting to make good on the promises Sarah made to the universe. I could dye my hair very blond and drive a truck. I could go to therapy and figure out her relationship to our father. I could read all the books and

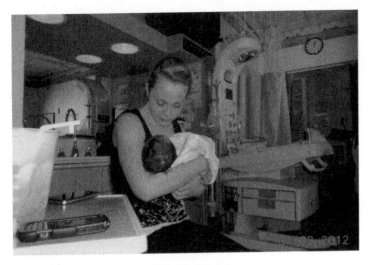

Holding Noelle's baby

take up painting and meet a nice man who loves me more than I love him. I could have a baby.

I still sometimes imagine holding a baby, let the thought slow my racing heart. But as time passes, the image of that baby becomes less and less my own. I'm not imagining some future child but rather remembering the first time I held Sarah.

I was five years old when my father placed her in my arms. She wailed and put her head against my chest.

Lynn, Sponsor

A month after Sarah told me she thought she could change her life by having a baby, things started to disappear: Sharon's pain pills, $500 from my wallet, our cars. Sarah claimed she had errands to run, friends to meet. She would run to the grocery store in Sharon's white Volvo but not return until the next morning. She borrowed Tess's truck to take the short drive from their cabin to Sharon's house, and by the time she brought it back, the previously full gas tank was nearly empty. She would visit my mother but make an excuse to leave right away. My mother lamented how skinny she was, but still said Sarah looked like a young Kate Moss. When my money went missing, Sarah suggested I must have dropped it out of my purse on the walk down the hill to my car. She was sympathetic and spent an hour with me looking for it.

Sarah told Sharon and me that sober meant everything: no pot, no booze, no drugs. She told Tess and friends that sober meant no hard drugs. She told Tess she was worried

Sharon was taking too many pain pills, but then told Sharon she should ask for stronger pain medication. She told all of us she and Ryan were getting married, and started nodding off while showing me the engagement ring he was going to buy her online. She said she was exhausted, sick, on her period, suffering from anxiety attacks, working too much.

Tess found heroin in Sarah's wallet. Sarah claimed it was someone else's, said she was helping that person get clean by holding on to it. Things blew up when the three of us decided to talk to her together.

"You need to get help, let us help you."

"You can't live here if you are getting high."

"Do you think we are fucking stupid?"

"We are worried about you."

Her response was a tirade, a confusing jumble of half truths and accusations that no one believed in her. She held up her phone to me.

"Do you see this?" she screamed. "Every phone call is my sponsor, and I text her every day." She was right; I could see that "Lynn, Sponsor" was on her call log, over and over again. "Would I be talking to her if I wasn't clean?" She stomped outside to smoke a cigarette while Tess, Sharon, and I hovered in the living room, trying to figure out what to do next.

I went and sat with her. She blew smoke angrily toward the expanse of trees down below us. "You guys never fucking believe me."

"Would you believe me if you found coke in my purse and I said I was keeping it for a friend?" I asked gently.

A few years of sobriety and therapy had made me realize that I needed to work on my critical spirit. I was trying to fold tenderness into the way I loved my family.

"Yes," she said bitterly. "Because you are my sister." She gave a hacking cough. "Doesn't fucking matter, no one ever believes me. I'm the fucked-up one in the family, and no matter what I do, you guys will always think so."

I tried to stay calm. "I don't think you're a fuckup, Sarah, I think you're an addict. Which I get, remember? I'm sober, and I know how hard it is."

She snorted with derisive laughter. "Right, says the person who has never detoxed or gone to rehab."

"What can I do to help right now?"

"You can believe me."

I sighed. "I'm sorry, I can't do that."

"Then fuck you guys, and fuck this place."

. . .

Sarah drove off with a friend, furious with all of us. She texted me a day later that she was shooting up in a Motel 6 and that it was all my fault, since I hadn't believed she was clean. I picked her up, convinced her to try and detox at my house.

The first day, she lay on the couch, tossing and turning, trying to distract herself from the pain with bad TV. She told me she was craving Chinese food, and I ordered all her favorite dishes. She could only manage a couple bites before running to the bathroom, retching. Her legs shook, and I could see muscle cramps take over her body.

With Sharon

She took baths every hour or so; the hot water soothed her spasming body. She chain-smoked on my front porch and texted furiously on her phone. She was restless and angry. I sat next to her on the couch and took her hand. "If you die," I said, "it will ruin my life." She knew, she said, and turned away from the conversation.

By the third day, I had figured out her passcode so I could break into her phone. I scrolled through her messages, looking for any sign that Sarah had been using for as long as we suspected. Finding nothing, I guiltily clicked on a text thread between her and "Lynn, Sponsor." I realized that it wasn't her sponsor, it was simply what she had named her drug dealer in her phone.

Intervention

I cannot remember my sister's body. Her smell is gone to me. I do not recall the last time I touched her. I think I can almost pinpoint it: the day I asked her to leave my home after I figured out she had stopped detoxing and started shooting up again, all the while trying to sell my things to her drug dealer as I slept. When she left, she asked me for $20, and I told her that I would give it to her if she sent me a picture of a receipt to show me she spent the money on something other than drugs. "Thanks a lot," she said, sarcastically. I hugged her, maybe. So much hinges on that *maybe*, the haunting maybe of our last touch.

The last time I saw my sister was at an intervention at a shitty hotel in Small Town. Our family friend Debbie flew my stepmother and me there in her three-seater plane. The intervention was put together hastily by Sarah's friend Noelle, who called us a few days beforehand, asking us to come. There were little resources or time to stage it properly—we couldn't afford a trained interventionist to come. Noelle told us she was afraid Sarah was going to die. I agreed to fly with Debbie and Sharon because Small Town was far away from home and I didn't want to drive.

Debbie sat in the pilot's seat, and I sat next to her. My stepmother was tucked in the third seat, directly behind us. It wasn't until takeoff that I realized with my body what a terrible decision it was to fly. I am terrified of heights and extremely prone to motion sickness. I was not prepared for what it meant to be in a small plane.

I could feel the outside while inside the plane. The vibration of chilly wind permeated through the tiny door and gripped my lungs, heart, head. It would have taken very little effort to open the door and fall, an endless horrifying fall to most-certain death. From the first swoop into the air, my stomach twisted into a mean, malicious fist that punched at my bowels and throat. For the next hour I sat trembling, my eyes shut tight. Through every dip, bounce, and shake, I held back bile and silently cried.

When we landed, I lurched off the plane and threw up. I do not remember what color it was. My stepmom handed me a bottle of water and half a Xanax, and I sat, legs splayed on the runway, until I thought I could stand again.

My sister vomited when she died. She shit. She bled. How much is required to leave our body before we are properly, truly, thoroughly dead? I dreamed one night that I sat with my sister's dead body and tried to scoop all her bodily fluids back inside her. Everything wet was warm, but her body was ice-cold. I knew that if I could return this warmth to her, she would come back to life. My hands were dripping with her blood and excrement, and while begging her insides to return to her, I cried a great flood of mucus and tears. This I remember, while our last touch still evades me.

. . .

My sister was late to her intervention. Many hours late. Seven of us, all women, five of us in sobriety, sat in that hot hotel room, repeatedly texting and calling Sarah's boyfriend, Jack, to bring her to us. I realized later that he probably told her they were going to the hotel to get drugs.

The hotel room was also where Sharon, Debbie, and I would be sleeping that night. It held two queen-size beds, our small amount of luggage, and four chairs we had discreetly borrowed from the hotel's conference room. I sat on one of the beds, perched on the edge anxiously, trying not to make eye contact with anyone else. I didn't know many of the other people there.

When I told my mom about the intervention days before, I had immediately followed with "But you don't need to come." There were so many reasons. She has goats and donkeys, cats and dogs who needed to be taken care of. She didn't have a vehicle that could make the drive. She could write a letter, I said, and I would give it to Sarah. The truth was, I didn't feel like managing her now-acrimonious relationship with Sharon. I didn't want to have to take care of my mom, on top of managing Sarah's state of being. It occurred to me, sitting in this crowded, strange room, that I might have been wrong.

Sitting diagonally across from me was Sarah's close friend Noelle, who had organized everything. Sarah and Noelle had met in recovery, lived together at Ryan's family home, and become close friends. They had remained friends even when Sarah started using again. Helen, a fair-haired middle-aged woman who was not one of the people Sarah knew from recovery but rather the mother of one of Sarah's boyfriends, sat on the other bed. Sarah's last sponsor, Lynn, sat near me. I had to stop myself from telling her how Sarah had used her name on her phone. Sitting in one of the chairs was the woman who was going to run the intervention. I cannot remember her name now, even though I can easily recall the sound of her loud, grating voice.

The interventionist had worked at Shining Light Recovery, the rehab Sarah had been kicked out of about a year and a half before, and was the only person Noelle could find on short notice. She had run her fair share of interventions, she told us, but she made it clear that because she hadn't had the time to work with us beforehand, this wouldn't run like a proper intervention. She smelled like musty clothes and showed too many teeth when she laughed. She talked about when she used to drink, with a tone that sounded more like longing than regret. When she started to disclose private information about my sister's time in rehab, I clenched my hands into fists.

"I'm the one that threw her out," the woman said. "I mean, she's a good kid, but once I caught her in the showers with that other girl, she had to go." Someone else said something, but I couldn't hear anyone else in the room. "No sexual conduct," she continued. "The rules are there for a reason." She chuckled and took a swig from her generic-brand cola. I felt hot and ill, my insides still a mess from the plane ride. We waited two more hours, listening to the interventionist talk, until Jack texted to say they had just pulled up.

When my sister arrived, she walked into the room and announced loudly, "Oh fuck, here we go." Then she sat, thin, resentful, and sneering, her hands stuffed into the front pocket of her sweatshirt. *Oh fuck, here we go*, I thought. The interventionist didn't say much, in sharp contrast to her chattiness while we were waiting. She briefly explained the process; we would each have a chance to speak, and then Sarah could decide if she wanted to go to a detox center that night.

We went in turns, speaking to Sarah directly or reading from a letter. Everyone had a different story, a different memory to start what they had to say, but everyone ended the same way: "Please get help. We are afraid you are going to die." Sarah was stone-faced but crying silently. This was unusual. When Sarah cried, she was a wailer; we called it her monkey howl.

When we were younger, we watched the movie *Little Women* again and again. We would often fast-forward through Beth's death, but sometimes we would let the scene play out. We would curl up on our maroon couch and cry as Jo realized her younger sister had died. For a moment I wished for the two of us to be alone, watching *Little Women* for the hundredth time. I could almost feel her small head on my shoulder as she wailed, "Why did Beth have to die? It's not fair." She sat across the room and wouldn't make eye contact with me.

I addressed Sarah first with our mom's letter. I started, "My dear little fawn, I know that things have gone wrong and that you have lost your way." My voice cracked and I found I couldn't continue, so I passed it to Noelle to read instead. It felt wrong to hear my mother's words come out of Noelle's mouth. Sarah was crying. She needs her mom, I thought frantically.

When it came time to speak to her myself, my mind was blank. I was angry. I was angry that I had to fly in a shitty small plane and be in this shitty small room to convince my sister to care one-tenth as much about her life as we did. I was furious that she still had a smirk, even while crying, while we spoke to her. Mostly, I was angry because I knew nothing I could say could make her leave this terrible town I had driven her to years before, and come home. That somewhere in her story there was a mountain of my own mistakes that had helped lead us to this moment.

"Sarah, I know you are angry and think that we are all here to make you feel bad. But we are here because we love you and are worried you might die. I don't know what I would do if you died." My sister sat quietly and listened. "I believe you can have any life you want." I paused. "And I have to believe that I still know you enough to know that this isn't the life you want." The more I talked, the further away she seemed, until I trailed off and nodded to the next person to talk.

After we had all spoken, Sarah rejected our help. She told us she had a plan to stop using on her own. "I have a guy I can buy methadone from, and I am going to do it by myself." Methadone was used to treat opioid addicts; the drug reduced the physical effects of withdrawal, decreased cravings, and, if taken regularly, could block the effects of opioids. It can itself be addictive—it's also an opioid. By law it can only be dispensed by an opioid treatment program, and the recommended length of treatment is a minimum of twelve months.

"I have a guy I can buy five pills from," Sarah insisted, as if that was comparable to a licensed methadone center, as if what she was suggesting wasn't its own kind of dangerous.

"But honey," my stepmother said gently, "we are offering you help right now. You can go to a detox center tonight."

"Absolutely not. I am not going to go cold turkey." Sarah was perceptibly shaking as she said this, the trauma of her past withdrawals palpable in her body. "I don't know if I can trust you guys."

She gestured to my stepmom and me. "I felt really betrayed by what happened." The heroin in her wallet, the confrontation at Sharon's, Motel 6, breaking into her phone. "You guys don't understand. Every other time I've done this, I've done this for you, for my family." She sat up a little straighter. "For once in my life, it's time for me to be selfish."

It was all I could do not to slap her across the face. I wanted desperately to feel my hand sting from the contact, to see her cheek bloom pink, to see if anything could hurt her. She wasn't going to use methadone to get clean. She just wanted us to leave her alone.

I made an excuse about needing to buy earplugs to sleep that night and walked out. I did not hug her or look at her. I did not know I would not see her again. I did not know I would not remember our last touch. I did not know that the next time I held her body, it would be chips of bone and gritty ash in a small cardboard box.

Deadly

I once helped Sarah fill out a rehab intake form where she listed every drug she had taken and then wrote about her experience with that drug. When we got to meth, she had wrinkled her nose. "I only did it once and I hated it," she told me. She didn't like how her thoughts raced, that she couldn't sit still. Meth use in the United States decreased in the early 2000s, when Congress passed several laws making it very difficult to manufacture meth in the country. But recently Mexican drug cartels have smuggled in an unprecedented amount of meth and are selling it for as low as $5 a hit.

When we got to heroin on the form, she said she couldn't count how many times she had taken it. She wrote that opioids made her feel calm and safe and numb. Humboldt County has unusually high instances of opioid and methamphetamine abuse, topping California counties in fatalities and babies born with addiction issues.

. . .

Sarah died of a lethal meth overdose. The coroner said it was many times over the recreational amount. According to the Centers for Disease Control and Prevention (CDC), a little over ten thousand people died this way in 2017, almost triple the number of meth-related fatalities in 2012.

I had been preparing myself for the call for years. I knew how addictive and dangerous opioids were. I had read memoirs and articles and statistics. She will most likely die from a heroin overdose, I told myself. Around forty-seven thousand people died from opioid overdoses in 2017, a number that has also risen consistently since 2012. I was not prepared for meth. I asked the coroner again and again if she was sure she was reading the right toxicology report. For a moment, I believed that she had the wrong girl, that Sarah might still be alive. It was one thing for Sarah to be killed by her friend, and another for her to be killed by a stranger.

RURAL, USA—On Monday morning, Otis Watts, local hunter, reported finding a leg and hand near an access trail in Dry Hills. Sheriff's officials responded to the scene and a search began to try and recover more of the body.

Watts was adamant that the injuries he saw weren't the result of wildlife trauma. "I've been hunting my whole life and no animal can make cuts like that. This was done by a person," he told reporters.

By Tuesday afternoon, investigators had found a torso, an arm, and two feet, said Sgt. Michael Green. "We have found the remains of a white male, late twenties to early thirties. At this point in time, we believe there to be only one victim but the search continues."

Major Crimes was called in Tuesday morning. The identity of the victim is unknown but police are hopeful that fingerprint or DNA evidence will yield a name. Green confirmed that this was being treated as a homicide investigation.

Watts said the area is typically quiet. "Things like this just don't happen here, so we are all pretty shocked."

Belief

Sarah believed in fairies. When she was little, she tromped with Tess, her best friend since age five, through the woods behind our stepmother's house and looked for signs of magic. Sarah told Tess that she was a fairy herself. That she had a psychic connection to the fairy queen and served as a messenger to the humans. Tess asked Sarah for proof, for some sign that she was telling the truth. Sarah sighed sadly and told her, "I could show you my wings, but if I do, I will die." When she was feeling more magnanimous, she told Tess that she would sacrifice herself, if it meant Tess believed.

They built fairy houses, small intricate palaces of wood, leaf, and flower. Even now, one of us will come across these long-forgotten altars, these shrines to magic. They appear so fragile and eerily permanent all at the same time, as if they are saying, *We will remain long after you are gone.*

Once I was up late talking to a boy, and I could hear Sarah and Tess giggling and whispering in the loft above my bed. It was past midnight. The rest of the house was quiet except for the chestnut tree outside dropping fruit onto the wooden deck. I ignored the noises above and shyly flirted into the phone. After our goodbyes, my face burning hot and my body throbbing painfully from hormones, I snuck the phone back to its cradle in the living room. It was only then that I noticed the smell.

I climbed up the ladder stairs to the loft. As the room came into view, there was a fierce spitting noise, and all I could see was fire. The girls had made an altar, taken

every candle in the house and lit them all, whispering prayers and spells into the smoke and flame. The individual flames had joined together and created a monstrous, beautiful pillar of light and heat.

I slid back downstairs and rushed to get something to help put the fire out. I could hear the girls' whispers turn to urgent calls for my help. I grabbed a large glass of water from my bedside table and a beach towel that was hanging over the back of a chair. With a splash and a smother, the fire was put out, and we were left with a wet, waxy mess.

The next day, after adults found out what they had done, Sarah and Tess spent hours with butter knives, trying to gently scrape all the candle wax off the furniture, floors, and wood.

There is still a scorch mark on the wall, the gray imprint of two girls who believed in miraculous things.

The Call

Seconds before the phone rings, my stepmother hands me a Fudgsicle. We stand in a small patch of light near the bathroom. She is in her nightgown, her short hair sticking up all over the place. She looks like a kid. "You really could be one of the Little Rascals," I say, laughing. Sharon smiles and yells out "Otay!" as she turns to leave. The phone starts to ring, and we both walk down the hallway to see who it is. The caller ID shows an area code that could only mean my sister. Sharon groans.

"You're it," I say, one foot turned to leave the room. "Just tell me she is alive." I say this every time there's a call that could be Sarah. I hear Sharon say hello.

"Jack? Jack?" she says. "Slow down, what happened?" Something about her voice makes me pause in the doorway.

I ask, "She's alive, right? Sharon?"

There is a noise that comes out of her. Then there are only fragments.

A book flies across the room.

Sharon asks if the paramedics can revive her.

My Fudgsicle, unopened, melts in its white plastic bag.

Jack wails through the phone.

"He thinks she's been dead awhile. Her body—"

Her body. She has turned from my sister into a body.

Initial grief is so very loud. It fills up your head with a roaring, hapless noise. I can't remember how my lungs work. The universe contradicts the body when someone dies.

Sharon hangs up the phone. For a moment I do not recognize her. Her face is grotesque with grief; her skin is gray, and her eyes are unfocused. Seeing her forces me back into my body; I cannot flee somewhere outside myself. There are things to do. I go up to her and hug my body against her shaking one. I take her by the shoulders.

"You can't hurt yourself," I command. She looks at me blankly. She is no stranger to suicidal ideation. "I mean it," I say. "I can't do this if you die." When she doesn't respond still, I place my hands on her chest and throat and let her feel my trembling skin. "You have to promise me you won't kill yourself."

"Okay," she finally says, "I promise I won't." She takes my hands off her chest and holds them. "It's all on you now." She was just two years younger than me when her own sister died. Death has followed Sharon ever since. She knows that I alone will hold the weight of my family.

A heaviness presses against what is left of my heart. My mother is at her home, miles away from this house in the woods. She has no idea her daughter is dead. I will need to be the one to tell her.

The Messenger

It takes over an hour to get to my mother's house. My partner is driving, even though I get carsick when I am a passenger. I cannot remember how to steer or shift gears. My dog, Charlotte, sits between us. The dark trees and mountain roads that I normally find soothing have turned against me. I have spent my life wanting my mother to be unequivocally proud of me. I have failed her.

Now I am the messenger that will shatter her being. I will be the unholy thing that snuffs out the divine light that was my sister. My mother will be left to face a darkness that I cannot begin to understand. Sarah is dead, and I am the daughter that remains, guilty of still breathing.

The truck makes a sharp turn, and I try to fight off the nausea that has moved out of my stomach and into my throat. I cannot tell if it is drizzling or if fog has crept in. Things don't look like they are supposed to. This is a copy of a world that existed just moments ago. *Take me back to the before. I will give you anything I have, all my gold and gifts and words. I will erase every future page to return to my old life.*

There is an alternate universe where I am the protector; I hold the head of the slayed beast high, and my family cheers, for I have saved them all. This is not that place. This is the place of ruin and stories that will end with *and then she died.* What good am I? I cannot even build a time machine. I should have studied science. I should have been a great many things. Now I am a sister without a sister, a daughter with a terrible task.

We are close. I look at my hands, and they appear monstrous. I wonder if anyone else will be able to see what I have become. The truck turns down the gravel driveway. I can see headlights on at the end of the road. She is in her car, about to leave to see friends or buy milk or watch a movie. She is about to do anything but hear the news I have to tell her.

I get out of the truck. She leaves the headlights on and opens the door. I go through the gate. I hear her before I see her.

"Rose?" she says.

"Yes, it's me."

"What's wrong? What happened?" I don't respond or move forward, and I can feel her worry grow. "Is it Charlotte? Did she die?" I look back at my sweet dog, who is still in the truck, her small face visible even through the light rain.

"No, it's not Charlotte." I walk to my mother. I look at her and wish I could make the next moment stretch infinitely, stand here forever until the sun has burned out and other galaxies have formed and the death of one girl will be inconsequential because we will all have perished.

"What is it?" she asks.

"Mom," I say. "It's Sarah. She's dead."

. . .

And in five words, I undo a life.

After

My sister and I had the same face. Our mother confuses our baby pictures. Sometimes I take photos of myself, and for a brief moment, I think my sister is still alive.

. . .

I am in charge of figuring out what to do with her body. I call mortuaries recommended by the coroner and send the body to be cremated. Sometimes it is *her* body, other times it is *the* body. I don't know which one feels worse.

. . .

There is a Christmas present, still wrapped, from the hopeful time before. I can't remember what is inside, only that I bought it a few weeks before she died, on the small chance she would be speaking to us by December. What do you do with a gift that no longer has a recipient?

. . .

I do not want to drive to pick up her ashes. There is an option to have them shipped. When the postwoman delivers them, I wonder if she knows she is handing me the wreckage of a life. I have to sign for the package.

. . .

I cannot talk about my mother's face after I told her Sarah was dead. It is knotted deep in my chest. I am afraid that if I untie it, I will unravel completely.

Remains

There is a potential life that I can never go back to. There is that life where the phone doesn't ring that night. I get up and have too much coffee. I worry a little bit every day about Sarah, I am mad at a lot of the choices she makes. It's there, in the back of my mind, when I go to the courthouse to legally marry my partner.

In this life, though, on the day I had planned to sign my marriage certificate, I go to the beach with my family and a few close friends and scatter my sister's ashes where the mouth of a river meets the ocean. My mother and I stand in the water and shake her remains into the sea. My sister and I stood in the same spot a few years before, to watch the vestiges of our father drift away.

We send flowers down the river with her. I watch them float away and think, I will never be able to choose flowers for my wedding without remembering this moment. I won't be able to look at peonies, roses, or lilies and not feel the weight of her ashes against my chest.

It is a lot to lose. Both of our potential lives.

Bargaining

I want to throw a party. The biggest party the world has ever seen. I would invite everyone, but only 0.000000001 percent would be able to come. We would take over all the beaches. We would become sand and sweat and song.

There would be DJs and drums and speakers that sat on the cliff tops and made the rocks shudder. We would dance and jump, and the ground would shake. We would become the world's largest heartbeat, a vibration that went from the shore to the sea. A tremor so strong that the ocean would have no choice but to give her ashes back. An energy quake that reconfigured the laws of physics and time and space until she was made whole again.

Sarah loved a good party.

Package

My mother dreams that my sister is cold. She wakes from this dream and drives to Target to buy my sister warm clothing: sweaters, long-sleeved shirts, leggings lined with fleece. She packs up the clothes and mails them, priority. The box travels many miles. It is delivered to my sister's house and left on her front porch because no one comes to the door when the postman knocks.

The postman must hear the dog barking. I wonder if he rushes away, busy and unbothered, or if he pauses, listening to the concerned wail of the animal inside. Does he knock again? Does he walk away with an aching, uneasy feeling in his chest? It will be four days before someone comes and finds them: the dog who will not be able to sleep alone anymore, and the girl who has overdosed.

In the weeks after her death, I google: *How does it feel to die of a meth overdose?* It occurs to me that everyone who truly knows is already dead. I believe things get quite warm when the body encounters too much meth. *An explosion, brain bursting, head blasting off.* These are the phrases that I read on drug forums. All that heat and then nothing. Or perhaps there is something in between the heat and the nothing. Maybe Sarah looked down from that in-between place and saw the lovely, beastly universe shimmering beneath her and said, "No, thank you. I am done with this."

The coldness comes later. So much cold; the bathroom tiles she dies on, her skin as the days wear on, my mother realizing she has sent a package to her already-dead daughter, the part of my heart where all the bad things live. I keep them encased in ice so they cannot touch me. At the very center of this lies the darkest part of me. It is slowly thawing. I can hear the *drip, drip, drip* of the icy memories that I fear will eventually drown me.

The box of warm clothing is thrown away, unopened. I hold on to the image of Sarah's shitty porch, with the white priority-mail box, waiting to be found. It sits, expectantly, as the dog tries to claw through the bathroom door, as her boyfriend finds her body, as the police come and go, as she is taken to the coroner. The box is thrown away, but the shitty porch remains.

My mother does not send packages anymore.

Moth

I play the lottery. I buy scratchers and scrape mounds of silver shavings onto the floor of my car. I buy SuperLotto, Mega Millions, and Powerball tickets. I play her birthday, the day she died, the day our father died. I hope I don't win. That would mean she is truly dead, and the universe has turned my grief to gold. I hope I do win. I am owed a cosmic debt, after all; I loaned Sarah so much money when she was alive.

One night, as Sharon sat in the dark of her living room, resting in her bitter grief, she had a sudden, urgent feeling that Sarah was there. She tells me this over the phone, the edge of heartache in her voice lifting as she speaks. At Sharon's, I cry and watch for signs that Sarah is present in some small way. I sit outside under a cedar tree and try to convince myself that the moth flying around my head is sending me messages from the other side, a Morse code of fragile, fluttering wings.

I stand in a store that sells Christmas ornaments, buying one for my mother, the only present we've agreed to exchange this year. I stare at a glass icicle hanging on a tree and will it to move. *If you are okay*, I tell her, *move the ornament. If you are okay, make the icicle tremble.* The cashier rings me up. The ornament is stubbornly still.

My mom finds shiny dimes in weird places: the middle of a freshly mopped floor, in a coffee cup that is used daily, on top of a high bookshelf. She thinks it is Sarah, for the dimes are often from the year she was born and always bright, like they are newly made. We joke that Sarah needs to step it up, send us a million dollars. The following week, my mom sends me a photo of a fake million-dollar bill sticking out of her mailbox. She is convinced I put it there.

My magical thinking is nightmares. I don't feel the hovering ghost or find shimmering dimes. I sit on Sharon's back porch in my crying chair and weep into the dense, quiet forest. Sarah has nothing for me. The moth flies away.

. . .

I only see Sarah when I sleep. I dream I spot her walking down the street. I suspect she is in witness protection, and I must break into her home to catch her changing, so I can see if she has the same tattoos. I confront her and slam her small body into a giant mirror that shatters as I wake up. In another dream, one that repeats, Sarah is alive and

I am the only person who knows she is about to die. I plead with her, tell her I have foreseen her death. I tell our parents. I hide her drugs, and I tie up her dealer in the trunk of my car. Nothing works. The last thing I see before the dream ends is her body.

Pause

I know what I am doing. I am curating her life. I take your hand and lead you through the blood and bile this story is made of. *Let me tell you how my family ended up here*. Here, in the place of small, dead feet balanced on the edge of grief. Here, in the land of maybe-murderers. Here, in the place of unknowable death, where I write every version of her last breath.

I place her cold corpse in the palm of my hand and show you. *See how small she is?* I close my hands and bring them to my mouth. You hear me blow warm air into the gap my fingers make. When I open my hands, for a brief moment you think she is alive again, her body glimmers in a way that tells you there is hope. *It is a trick of the light*, I tell you, gently. I cannot bring the dead back to life.

The unbearable note of grief still sings in my head. The melody of which you will never hear.

SMALL TOWN, USA—Investigators say there's a connection between the gunshot victims at Little Tree Trailer Park and the remains found in Dry Hills. The deceased man, whose body parts were scattered in the Dry Hills region, has been identified as 28-year-old Leland Miller.

Dale Brady, 32, has been arrested in connection with both crimes while Raymond Douglas, 33, has been charged only in connection to the Leland Miller killing. According to Sheriff's officials, they believe Leland Miller was present during the Little Tree robbery and homicides.

County investigators said Brady shot and killed Clayton Sparks, 32, and Lindsey Levy, 29, when Sparks interrupted Brady and Miller robbing a trailer. Brady then went into Levy's trailer and shot her.

Leland Miller witnessed both murders.

A little more than two weeks later, officials responded to a report made by a local hunter who had stumbled upon human remains, which were later identified as belonging to Miller.

On January 23, 2014, Brady was arrested by detectives on outstanding warrants. Douglas was arrested almost a month later.

On Wednesday, both Brady and Douglas were arraigned for different charges in the respective homicides. It is believed that Brady is negotiating a plea deal to avoid the death penalty while Douglas has pled not guilty.

PART IV

The Man

Facebook

I am on Facebook and see a post by Noelle: "My best friend will never get justice and they may never be held responsible for her but one day after their long miserable lives they will answer to someone!" I pause. I reread. The only person I have ever heard Noelle refer to as her best friend is Sarah. I comment with a question mark. She responds: "I'll call u."

She calls a long fifteen minutes later. "There is a rumor going around that Sarah might have been given a hot shot."

"A hot shot?" I ask.

"It's an intentional overdose."

"I don't understand," I say blankly.

"Well, that man I told you about, who was with Sarah on the day she died. He is involved in some heavy shit." This man—his name is Ray—had admitted to Noelle that he had picked Sarah up that final morning and taken her to get heroin. He said he dropped her off at Jack's house while he ran an errand, and when he returned, she didn't answer the door.

"What kinds of things is he involved in?" I ask.

"It's not just what he is involved in. It's what Sarah got into too." Noelle sighs and goes quiet.

"What did she do?" Noelle doesn't answer right away, and my voice cracks as adrenaline floods my system. "What did she do?"

Reluctantly she tells me what little she knows: Sarah gave or sold a shotgun to some drug friends. Two people were murdered in a robbery gone wrong. Two weeks later someone else was killed, and Ray was involved.

"I still don't know how this has anything to do with Sarah, other than the gun . . ." I trail off. Is this who Sarah had become, someone who provided a gun used to kill people? I realize I should be taking notes or keeping track of what Noelle is saying.

"Someone told me that Ray and Dale started to freak out about getting caught, so they were trying to tie up loose ends."

"And?"

"Sarah was a loose end."

. . .

As soon as I hang up with Noelle, I'm online, in research mode, looking up every name she gave me until I find the news articles. I print everything out and sit down to highlight, circle, and annotate. The story comes into focus.

. . .

There are three main people involved: Raymond Douglas, Dale Brady, and Leland Miller.

I don't recognize Ray, but his picture frightens me. He is short but muscular with dirty blonde hair and a strong chin. When I look at him, I feel queasy. He has been arrested, accused of killing a man, Leland Miller, and then dismembering his body.

I recognize Dale Brady immediately: he is covered in tattoos, a white power symbol inked on his forearm. He is at the center of this case. He is accused of killing a couple at a trailer park during a robbery gone wrong. He has been charged, alongside Douglas, in the death of Leland Miller, who was reportedly present for that initial robbery and double homicide. Brady was worried that Miller would talk to the police. He was a liability.

. . .

It occurs to me that there is a fourth person involved: Sarah. The gun used to kill the couple belonged to Sarah's boyfriend, Jack. She had given it to Brady right before the homicides took place. Or sold it. Maybe she sold it for drugs. Maybe she knew what the gun would be used for. Or she figured out afterward that her good friend Dale had murdered two people with the weapon she had handed to him.

Jack was angry when he figured out the gun was missing; it had belonged to his grandfather. He confronted

Sarah about it, and she confessed to him that Brady had it. Jack called Brady and told him to return the gun, or he would go to the police and tell them that Brady was in possession of a stolen firearm. At the time, Jack had no idea that the gun had been used in a double murder; he just wanted it back. It was returned to him, sawed off, and he tucked it away where even Sarah wouldn't be able to find it. Since all this has come to light, he has given it to the police.

This is what Jack says to me on the phone. He is hard to get ahold of, and reluctant to tell me anything. He is no longer in California, having fled to a different state because he has heard through friends that, because of his connection to this gun and Sarah, he could be the next person killed. He tells me that the house was ransacked the day he found her body. He tells me that Douglas has put a hit on him, and I try not to laugh. It sounds ridiculous to me, like a shitty *Law & Order* episode that can't seem to wrap up by the end of the hour. But the fear in Jack's voice, the newspaper articles, this terrible Tattooed Man who called Sarah his sister, the fact that Ray was the last person to see her alive—it's all starting to paint a very different picture of what happened in the early morning of November 19, 2013.

Psychic

The first time I went to see Lillian, a clairvoyant reader and self-proclaimed metaphysical teacher, was a few years prior to Sarah's death. A friend had given me a session with her. I had gone mainly just to know what it was like to see someone who claimed they had supernatural gifts. One of the first things she told me was that my family of origin was like a black hole for me.

She had also told me that Sarah and I were connected throughout time. In one past life, she said, Sarah had been my baby, and we were trapped in a building that was on fire. Lillian had an image of me standing at a third-floor window, throwing my child to the crowd below, saving Sarah's life before I burned to death.

"I see you walking down a long road," she had said. "There is a misshapen boulder that you are rolling alongside you with a long wooden stick. You take it with you everywhere you go." I hadn't been able to look at her as she said this; it had felt intrusive and true, this image of me she had conjured. "You see," she continued, "that boulder is everything bad you think you have done or you think you are. And most people, once they make amends or change a behavior, they let go of those things, but you, you tend to them, you keep them with you."

My first experience with her didn't convince me she was psychic, but I did think she was intuitive and articulate.

. . .

In the weeks following Noelle's Facebook post about Raymond, I have been trying to put together as much as I can of what happened to Sarah. But I have gleaned everything I can from newspaper articles and social media; I am far away from where Sarah died; Jack has stopped answering the phone. The same friend that sent me to Lillian the first time suggests I return to her to ask about my sister's death. I am equally skeptical and hopeful. Maybe Lillian will intuit some concrete next step for me, help me sort through the noise that has been keeping me up at night.

. . .

Lillian is dressed in ill-fitting polyester pants and a brown long-sleeved shirt with several stains on it. Sitting there, eyeing her clothes, I wonder if this was the best choice. I don't want the psychic to tell me that my sister loves me and that everything is going to be okay. I am not ready to be comforted. I've already paid for the session, though, so

I hand her a blank CD to record my reading, and I try to stop being so judgmental about her clothes. My face turns red with the effort of trying to think of anything else. On the off chance she is clairvoyant, I don't want her knowing what I think of her pants.

Lillian isn't a crystal-ball psychic. The reading takes as long as is needed: my first one was close to three hours. She doesn't look at palms or use tarot cards. Instead, she closes her eyes and reaches out to her "guidance" (what she calls it) to communicate your questions and concerns, and then shares what she finds out with you.

This session starts off as my first one did; she asks me why I am there and what I want guidance on. I explain what I have heard about my sister: the gun she sold, the people who were involved, the possibility that she was killed. Lillian likes to see photos of the people her clients are coming in to talk about, so I pull up the pretrial photos from the news and show her Raymond, Dale, and Leland. I show her pictures from Sarah's Instagram, taken in the months before she died, where she looks too thin and smiles indifferently.

I sit across from Lillian, and she closes her eyes, looking relaxed, as she starts the process of communicating with her guidance. She stays this way for several minutes until, with a sharp intake of breath, she balls her hands in tight fists. She is in this state, agitated, for another few minutes before opening her eyes. It isn't until she is looking at me again that I realize I am crying.

Lillian takes a deep breath before speaking. "I called for her, for Sarah, and I talked to her." I wrinkle my nose at this—the reason why I have come, and the thing I don't really believe can happen. She continues, "I really debated with her—we went back and forth over whether this is what she wanted to say to you, if this is how she wanted to say it, but she is insistent."

"What did she say?"

"Three times she said to me, 'That bastard Raymond fried me.'" Fried me? I had seen that phrase as I read through hundreds of drug forums, trying desperately to understand how my sister's last moments felt.

"What happened?"

"I asked her that. She kept saying, 'He fried me.' She said, 'He told me it was really good stuff and then . . .'" Lillian stops.

"And then?"

"And then she said, 'It was like the top of my head blew off.'"

We sit with this, these strange, sickening words coming out of the mouth of this woman who is old enough to be my mother. Has she ever heard someone talk like this before? Does she know what a meth overdose feels like? My mouth feels dry. There is no such thing as a psychic.

But the psychic goes on. "Sarah wanted me to say: 'Tell them I'm going to be there when they stick a needle in his arm, laughing.' She is angry."

"She's feisty," I reply, dumbly.

"She's hostile."

"I don't blame her."

"I got an image of her with her legs crossed, sitting on a gurney, while he was strapped down, ready to be executed."

Somehow this image is more vivid than any I have conjured of Sarah's death, accidental or otherwise. "She's convinced he needs to pay."

Lillian stops for a moment to hand me tissues. I blow my nose, loudly. Lillian waits. She starts to speak again. "She is sorry that she made such a mess. She wasn't trying to die."

I turn that phrase over in my head: *wasn't trying to die.*

Was she trying *not* to die?

What is the difference?

"Is she mad at me?"

"No."

"We just hadn't talked in so long."

"I told her that you would be talking to your mom about this, and was there anything she wanted to say . . ."

"And?"

"'Just tell Mom I'm sorry I fucked up so much.'"

The Man

Ray starts getting texts from her before the sun has even risen. He has been up all night, pacing his small house while chain-smoking cigarettes. He wants to get high but needs a clear head. Sarah texts him again: *r u up?*

Fuck it, he thinks, and tells her he is on his way over. He drives his truck the five miles to her house. It is still dark out, and he can just barely see the fog of his warm breath hitting the cold air. He doesn't bother knocking; he knows her boyfriend is out of town. She is antsy, clearly in need of a fix.

She follows him out to the car. As they drive, he lets her change the radio station. When they pull up, he tells her to wait in the car. She hands him some money, a crumpled pile of ones and fives, saying she can get him more later. He nods and goes into the house. This time he knocks.

He talks to the guy inside quietly, the TV blaring in the background. He hands him the money and tucks the small baggie filled with white powder into his jacket pocket. His truck is still running, and he holds his hands up to the heating vents for a minute before putting the vehicle in reverse. As they drive, he pulls out the baggie and waves it to her teasingly.

"China white?" she says, her voice perking up. "Fuck, man. It's not my birthday."

"A treat," he says, and puts it back in his pocket.

. . .

Back at her place, she lets her dog out to piss while she gathers up everything they need: the ribbon, the spoon, the ball of cotton, the needle, the cup of water. She holds up a lighter, but he shakes his head. "Nah, this shit's too pure to need heat."

They sit down in the bathroom, up against the wall. She asks if he wants to go first, but he shakes his head. She looks relieved. He knows what she likes; they have done this many times before. She stretches her leg out a little, and he takes the red ribbon and ties it around her thigh. She is so skinny now. He preferred it when she had tits, but whatever. He measures out the drugs, tapping the powder into the spoon, looks at her, then taps out some more.

She hums a little as he prepares it, watching as he swishes the water into the powder until it is dissolved and then sucked up into the syringe. He finds a good vein on the back of her knee. His hands tremble a little as he slides the needle in. He pulls back the plunger until he sees a bit of blood. She closes her eyes, waiting expectantly. He hesitates, and she opens her eyes: "What's up?"

"Nothing," he says, and pushes the plunger down.

It takes her a few seconds to react. "What the fuck?" she says, eyes going wide, jaw tightening. "This isn't fucking dope," she chokes out. He doesn't respond, just stands and takes a step back. She puts her hand to her chest, scratching at her sternum frantically. Her skin is already taking on a bluish tint. She tries to push herself up from the floor but collapses back against the wall.

She tries to talk, letting out a rattling noise that he thinks might mean: *Why?* He doesn't like watching this. He likes her. He was just cleaning up a mess that no one else would handle. He has to make sure it takes.

Her eyes look like they have their own heartbeat. They pulse angrily at him while her face widens into a grimace. He kneels down. "Fuck," he says. "Nothing personal." He's pretty sure Dale told her about the fight two weeks ago, the knife, the blood, the body that he turned into pieces. *She'd fucking snitch*, he tells himself. *She's never even been to jail.*

He stands back up as her body starts to seize. She's so thin, she looks like a broken doll. He picks up the needle and wipes the syringe down with his shirt. He tosses it next to her twitching legs. He walks around her; he can't look at her anymore. He closes the door behind him.

He waits a minute, listening. He hears the vomit try to come out, the cough and gargle of her seizing throat choking. It gets quiet for a moment, and then he can hear her body slide sideways, hitting the door.

He has shit to do now. He starts to search the house for anything that might incriminate him or Dale. He can't find the shotgun she let Dale use: her boyfriend must have it. He pulls apart closets, throwing coats and clothes onto the floor. He can't find any of the stolen shit; she must have pawned it. He pulls out drawers, picks up sofa cushions, and throws them in frustration when he finds nothing. He goes to the couch and grabs her purse. He looks through her phone and quickly deletes all his messages to her. He looks through her wallet—no more cash, but a stolen credit card that he pockets.

He can't be sure that no one knows they went to get shit this morning. He grabs a paper napkin from the kitchen and writes a note. "Came back—no answer! Where the fuck are you? Txt me." Her dog has started to sniff and paw at the bathroom door. He looks at Ray and a growl rips through the room.

Fuck this, he thinks, and leaves, the house in shambles from his search, the dog clawing more urgently at the door, the body in the bathroom so very still now. He locks the door behind him and leaves his note.

His truck takes a second to start, and his heart jumps around before the engine finally turns. He needs some booze, a cigarette, and a couple hours' sleep.

Letter

Sgt. Bickel
Rural Police Department
Small Town, USA

Dear Sgt. Bickel,
I am writing you in regard to a telephone conversation I had with you a few weeks ago about my sister Sarah Andersen, who died on November 19, 2013, of a methamphetamine overdose. She was found on November 22, 2013, in the home of her boyfriend, Jack Edwards. You asked us to send a statement regarding information that has come forward concerning the possibility of Sarah's death being a murder by Raymond Douglas.

We are concerned with the possibility that she was murdered because of what she knew about the triple homicide that involved Raymond Douglas, Dale Brady, and Leland Miller. We love Sarah very much and want to be an advocate for her, should the rumors we have heard be true. We understand that this is all hearsay, but we hope that you will look into it. Sarah was a smart, beautiful 24-year-old woman who made some bad choices at the end of her life, including her relationship with Raymond Douglas and her friendship with Dale Brady, but the heart of Sarah was good and kind. She deserved better than what happened to her. We appreciate any help you can give in this matter. We hope that you keep in contact with us regarding anything that comes up in regards to her death. Please use Rose Andersen as the primary contact. Thank you for your help.

Attached is a written report of everything that has been told to us.

Sincerely,
Rose Andersen

Report

*W*ritten *report regarding the death of Sarah Andersen, age 24*

The following was told to us by Noelle Brooks:

About a month after Sarah's death, ███████████ contacted and shared information with Noelle concerning Raymond Douglas and Dale Brady. ███████████ claimed that Sarah had found out that the gun she had sold to Dale Brady had been used in the murders of Clayton Sparks and Lindsey Levy on October 18, 2013. It is possible that Sarah also found out about the details surrounding Leland Miller's death, which occurred sometime in early November.

███████████ said he had been present at a conversation with Raymond Douglas and Dale Brady in which Ray said Sarah needed to be taken care of because of what she knew. Ray wanted to know if she had told anyone about the homicides and expressed interest in looking at her phone to see if she had said anything. In this conversation, Dale Brady stated that he would handle Sarah, that nothing needed to happen to her, but it appeared that Ray disagreed. ████████████ also said that two other women had been severely beaten and hospitalized because of what they knew in regards to the murders. ████████████ came forward with this information because, he said, he had always liked Sarah and was upset about what happened to her.

Noelle told us that Sarah met Dale Brady in AA. They became close in sobriety and stayed friends when they each relapsed. Dale wrote on her Facebook page that when he found out who did this to her, "they would pay." In a letter written to Noelle from prison, Dale stated that he believes Ray is responsible for Sarah's death.

Noelle examined Sarah's phone and figured out that Ray was the last person with her the morning she died. The following is what Ray told Noelle about that morning. He picked Sarah up to take her to get a gram of heroin and then dropped her back off at her house. He then left to run an errand, and when he returned, Sarah did not answer the door. He left her a note on the door and left.

We are struggling to understand why Ray says he took her to get heroin, but she died of a meth overdose. Why would he admit that he was the one to take Sarah to get drugs the day she died, but lie about the kind of drugs she bought?

. . .

The following was told to us by Jack Edwards:

Jack has told us that Sarah had a sexual relationship with Ray. In the three days prior to her death, Sarah had been primarily with Ray. When Jack looked at Sarah's phone after her death, there were at least five outgoing text messages to Ray. It was clear from the messages that Ray and Sarah were having a conversation; however, someone had wiped the phone of Ray's replies.

Jack left the state for a month to stay with family, fearing for his safety because of what he knew about Sarah and the gun. When Jack returned to Small Town, he told us that he was coming forward with this information but changed his mind because he is afraid he will be killed. When we offered to come forward instead, Jack said, "Good, they don't know where you live." Jack is no longer returning our calls or texts. We believe he is very scared.

This is the small amount of information that we have been able to gather on our own. We appreciate any help with this matter.

Portrait

I sit with my mom a year and a half after Sarah's death. She is telling me about her printmaking class. It is chilly outside the café, but the sun is bright and the air smells of rain.

"One of the guys in my class, his girlfriend had an abortion, and he is a wreck about it. He does all these really graphic prints with unborn babies and images of umbilical cords coming out of his body."

I listen but am distracted by a couple arguing next to us. I wish I could hear what they are saying, but I can't make out the words behind their furtive, tense whispers.

"Did you know I drew a portrait of Sarah when she was younger? I have a photocopy of it on my studio door," my mom continues, as if it makes perfect sense in conjunction with the story of her distraught printmaking friend.

"Oh yeah?" I say, more focused now that she is talking about Sarah.

"I realized that I don't have to draw her death in order to move on. I don't have to draw her murderer or create some terrible death scene to process all of this."

I stare at my mother's face as she says this. I wonder if Sarah's death is as evident in my body as it is in hers.

"That's good, Mom," I say, offering her a small smile.

"What I am trying to say"—she pauses, reaching out to grab my hand for a second—"is that you don't have to write the story of her death. Her story isn't your story. You don't have to make it yours. You can live your life. Her death doesn't have to take over everything."

. . .

I have a memory from when Sarah and I were kids, the two of us at the river. I must have been about eleven and Sarah five. We swam in the gentle water and lay in the sun until we turned pink. I buried her in the sand, and she laughed and I laughed until we were simply laughing about how long we had been laughing.

I can no longer think about this moment without thinking about the moment she died. That is what this death has done. It has taken my best moments and paired them with my worst thoughts. It changes the way I remember.

I look at my mom, part of me still pushing the sand over my little sister's sunburned legs, part of me wondering what Sarah's last thought was before she stopped breathing.

I try to focus on this moment: the smell of the rain to come; the chilly sun; the couple next to us, kissing now; my mom's coffee, still hot and steamy.

"Thanks, Mom," I say, looking down at the trembling poached eggs I haven't taken a bite of yet. I wish that she was right. That my grief didn't need this obsessive replaying of the past. I have become a scavenger, picking through scraps of memory. If I can reassemble Sarah's life, see every piece of her death, perhaps she will come back to me. She believed in magic once. Isn't this a kind of terrible magic?

My mother has given me a new memory. She has made this moment our perfect moment, which I will replay when I need to calm the hurricane of grief that follows me.

SMALL TOWN, USA—The last defendant involved in a string of murders in 2013 began standing trial on Monday.

Raymond Douglas, 31, is accused of killing Leland Miller. He faces 50 years in prison if convicted. His former co-defendant, Dale Brady, is expected to testify against him.

The multiple twists and turns in the case were outlined in opening statements Monday. Douglas is accused of killing Miller, 29, and cutting his body into parts before disposing of them in Dry Hills and other areas.

That investigation also linked Brady and Miller to the deaths of a couple who were killed in Little Tree Trailer Park only a few days before Miller was killed and dismembered.

Brady was sentenced in June 2014 to three consecutive life sentences with no possibility of parole after taking a plea bargain to avoid a potential death penalty sentence.

In his opening statements, District Attorney Phil Boyd said that Brady is cooperating fully and providing testimony on behalf of the prosecution. He says Brady will testify to Douglas's involvement in Miller's murder and the tense days leading up to that fatal night.

Shawn Cook, the defense attorney for Raymond Douglas, says his client is innocent.

Let Go

I hear nothing after I send off the report to the police department. I try to forget the toxicology report, the rumors that still circle online, the man's name. That man is going to trial for murder, I tell myself. It does not matter that I will never know if he had a hand in her death.

A year goes by. I dream of grad school, of leaving my partner, who has taken to sleeping in the other room, of doing something more than sitting in endless grief. I receive a phone call one April afternoon about a week before Raymond Douglas goes on trial for the murder of Leland Miller. It is a Detective Bud Hayes, calling to tell me that he has reason to believe my sister may have been killed.

"I know," I say. "I sent the police department this information a year ago."

"What?" He clears his throat loudly. "What did you send?"

I explain the Facebook post, my amateur investigation, the letter and report I sent. He asks me to re-send it all to him via email.

"I'm calling because someone came forward and provided us with information in regard to Sarah's death."

"Who?" I ask, even though I am sure it is Dale Brady.

"I'm not at liberty to say," he responds. "But I want you to know we are looking into the matter." I let out something between a sob and a breath. "We will do everything we can, but I don't want you to get your hopes up."

"Of course," I say.

"One more thing . . ." He hesitates. "I want you to know that Sarah's name might come up in Raymond's trial."

"The one that's about to start?"

"Yes, his lawyer seems to be working it into his defense case." Detective Bud Hayes sighs. "But I want you to know that no matter what, Raymond Douglas will be in prison for the rest of his life. There is no way he is walking away from this trial."

. . .

By summer 2015, the trial will be over. In a surprise turn, the primary witness for the prosecution, Dale Brady, will recant his testimony, and Raymond Douglas will be acquitted of all charges related to the murder of Leland Miller. He will be sentenced to seven years in prison for a handful of other charges unrelated to the Miller case.

Over the next three months, Detective Bud Hayes slowly tapers off his phone calls and emails. In one of our final conversations, he tells me that while he has suspicions that Ray was involved in Sarah's death, it will be almost impossible to prove. He won't tell me specifically what he has found during his inquiry because he needs to keep things "close to the chest."

. . .

My mother tells me that Raymond has become a ghost to her, that he will remain that way unless he is standing in front of her. She says, "He doesn't live in me." Sharon tells me she has to let go of her anger, of her hatred. She doesn't forgive him, she explains, but she can't live with him filling up her days anymore. I nod along, knowing that they are both the better for letting go.

. . .

And yet, and yet, and yet.

Need

I make every change I can think of: I apply to grad school, my partner and I finally break up, I address a number of health issues that have been hanging over me. I get into grad school and choose a small arts college outside Los Angeles. I fall in love with Josh, a funny, kind man who I meet in an improv group. I move to Southern California to spend two years reading and writing. Josh follows in a matter of months, and we move into a sweet one-bedroom apartment with our dog.

I read and reread any article I can find about Raymond's trial. There aren't many. I try to understand how Dale's recanted testimony came to be, who the different witnesses were, what evidence was presented, how Sarah's death was addressed.

I have Google alerts set for Dale Brady and Raymond Douglas. I search for Raymond Douglas in a Prison Inmate Finder until one day his name no longer appears.

I call the number listed and find out that he has been released early, after serving only a couple years of his sentence.

I have trouble accessing rage. It is hard for me to feel anger. I can settle into bleakness or dark grief, but I see that Raymond Douglas is no longer in prison and feel nothing. Or rather, I feel a blankness where rage should be.

Over time, the blankness becomes a gnawing thought, a need to know more.

I email Detective Bud Hayes; I call the sheriff's office; I order a copy of Sarah's coroner's report. I find out I can pay for a copy of the court transcripts from Raymond's trial, and $1,300 later, seventeen hundred pages weighing over twenty pounds are delivered to my apartment, bound into six volumes. I start to read. I look for my rage.

People v. Douglas

The trial transcript is equal parts dry (technical witnesses discussing how cell tower coverage works), disturbing (Watts describing the moment he finds Miller's leg), and emotional (Sarah's name, any mention of her).

While reading, I have moments when I cry out, press my hands on the page as if my touch can make the words disappear. My dog is startled by my outbursts. I rant to Josh as he makes me cup after cup of coffee to fuel my reading. I take fastidious notes, designate colored tabs for different parts I want to keep track of. I call my stepmom and tell her, haltingly, of the first time Sarah's name appears during the trial. I read over certain sections obsessively, imagining myself in the courtroom watching the witness on the stand. A transcript of a court hearing does not include stage directions or blocking, unfortunately, but the more I read, the more I feel as if I am there.

Dale Brady had a public defender who arranged for his plea deal. Raymond Douglas can afford his own lawyer:

Shawn Cook is a self-described "bulldog." Cook frightens me, like he could climb out of the transcript and convince me that I am guilty of all the crimes. He reminds me of my father, who could turn an argument on its head, coerce an apology instead of giving one.

From the first page of the prosecution's case, Cook comes out swinging: he implies evidence has been tampered with and suggests that witnesses are lying. He is actually quite good at his job.

The prosecution is led by District Attorney Phil Boyd. He is methodical and careful. I see him as an Atticus Finch type, an upstanding lawyer in the midst of a dysfunctional justice system. I don't know this, of course; I just need someone to be the good guy. Boyd seems confident in his case, lays out each piece of evidence as if he is showing a winning hand. Which makes sense; there is a coconspirator willing to testify against Douglas, multiple witnesses who can place Douglas at the scene the night Eric Miller was killed, cell records that determine that Douglas was at the house when the murder occurred and in the areas where body parts were dumped. When things begin to deteriorate, Boyd keeps his composure, even though I cannot. I throw the transcript on the bed and march into the kitchen to vent to my partner. "It's all falling apart," I tell him. "There is no way for the case to recover from this."

Dale Brady is the center of the deterioration. He gives multiple days of testimony for the prosecution. He was at the house; indeed, he participated in the murder of

Leland Miller. He names Raymond Douglas as his coconspirator.

The details of his testimony are horrific. Brady walks everyone through his version of the night of Miller's death. Douglas came up behind Miller while he was making a sandwich in the kitchen. Douglas picked up a knife laying on the counter and stabbed Miller in his side. An altercation ensued and Miller was stabbed multiple times. Brady claims he heard the noise from the fight and came running, saw Miller bleeding and weeping on the tile floor. Brady, in an act of self-described mercy, took the knife from Douglas and slit Miller's throat. Douglas and Brady brought the body into the garage and chopped Miller into smaller, more manageable pieces.

During Brady's cross-examination, defense attorney Cook brings up Sarah. "Do you believe my client is responsible for the death of one of your closest friends?" Brady is reluctant to discuss my sister but Cook is persistent. "Isn't it true that you want revenge against Raymond Douglas because you blame him for the death of Sarah Andersen and that is why you are testifying against him?" Cook says that Brady is doing all of this, lying about Douglas's involvement, so he can get him imprisoned as retribution. It goes on and on, a relentless barrage to break Brady. At one point it seems to be working, and he refuses to answer any more questions. He says that he doesn't care that he is violating an order from the court to answer Cook. After all, he will already be in prison for the rest of his life. After a recess, Brady agrees to come back to the stand, and he sticks by his story that Douglas is culpable in Miller's death.

. . .

Attorney Boyd rests his case. Cook is scheduled to take a number of days to present the defense. He calls two technical witnesses to the stand before announcing that Dale Brady will now be a witness for the defense. This is different from Cook calling Brady back to the stand to cross-examine him. This means that Brady is testifying on behalf of the defense to further their case instead of the prosecution's.

Is Cook smiling as he talks to Brady? Is he swaggering around the courtroom? Cook asks Brady a series of questions he has been asked before. This time, the answers are different. Brady takes full responsibility for Miller's death, erases Douglas's presence from the scene. He explains away his previous testimony as anger toward Douglas manifested as false accusation. His conscience will no longer allow him to say that Raymond Douglas was a killer.

. . .

Brady admits under Boyd's cross-examination that he was able to send a message through the jail the night before this testimony and communicate with Douglas. No one knows what was said. Was there a financial agreement made? A threat? Perhaps Douglas told him what he actually knew of Sarah's death. I suppose there is a chance that Douglas pleaded with Brady, and it changed his mind. One conversation floating through the jail has tainted an entire murder trial.

I hold my breath. Something as close to rage as I have felt during this process creeps into my body, a fury at Brady for changing his testimony and letting me down. Me, personally.

Boyd does his best to recover. He brings in video of Brady walking police through the scene of the crime early on. Brady is describing what he and Douglas did to Miller. He breaks down, weeping into his hands. Boyd's closing argument lays out every detail of the case, building a strong argument that Raymond Douglas is guilty of murder.

Cook's closing statement attempts to dismantle Boyd's version of events, but it is Brady's displays of feeling throughout his waffling testimony that are his main focus. Cook acknowledges that Brady's testimony is problematic, that he isn't trustworthy. He urges the jury, though, to look for the points where Brady shows genuine emotion in the courtroom. Therein lies the truth, Cook claims. "Dale Brady only showed emotion when he spoke about the death of his friend, Sarah Andersen. Brady blames Raymond Douglas for her overdose. That emotion, that anger, is what drove Brady to make false claims about my client's involvement in the death of Leland Miller."

. . .

Raymond Douglas is acquitted. A jury member cites Brady's lack of credibility as the deciding factor. I am stuck, reframing this trial scene, wondering how Sarah's death has been used by the defense to set her potential murderer free.

The Body

I run instead of write. I go to my apartment's gym and
listen to loud, throbbing music and run until the image
of her body is replaced with breathless black spots. If my
heartbeat slows too much or there is a break in the music,
she appears, her back on the tile floor and her feet resting
on the bathroom counter. For a moment she is laughing,
and I am next to her. I can feel her feet lean against mine.
Her socks are soft and gray, and they are warm against my
bare toes. I do not want to write this. The ending is always
the same: I am not there, she is not laughing, and her feet,
while still perched on the bathroom sink, are cold and
four days dead.

I have spent years conjuring her body, have envi-
sioned myself next to her as she died again and again.
And yet, in all of those versions, I never imagined her
with her back on the floor, feet balanced on the sink.
I never imagined the smallest details of her clothing,

black-and-gray-striped leggings, soft gray socks, layered blue and black tank tops. There is something called a "coroner narrative" that is included in the coroner's report. I was not expecting this when I ordered the report from the coroner's office. This is how I know the position of her body when she was found. And this knowledge, the exactness with which I can see her now, is shattering in its precision. We would lie like that as children, in the living room, our backs pressed against the carpet and our feet on the sofa.

The narrative included in the report is written by Lucy Gray, the coroner investigator who was called to the scene when my sister was found. It is a page, single-spaced, and details Lucy's movements through the house, what she saw, what she did, who she talked to. After initially being named in the report, Sarah is referred to as "the decedent" throughout. I read through this official story of my sister's found body and cannot help but think of that same evening, the phone ringing at my stepmother's house, and all that followed.

Before Lucy receives a call at her residence at 2010 hours to examine a deceased subject, my stepmother receives a call from Jack, who is hysterical, so loud that I can hear his tinny weeping from across the room. I make Sharon ask if Sarah can be resuscitated, not knowing she has been dead for days. When Lucy arrives at the house that holds my sister's body, I am holding my stepmother's shoulders over three hundred miles away, shaking out of her a promise not to hurt herself in response to Sarah's death. As Lucy walks into the house, down a hallway to the bathroom where the decedent is lying supine on the floor, I am on the phone with my therapist, incoherently asking her what to do next. While Lucy and an officer load the decedent into the body bag and secure her in the back of the coroner's vehicle, I am in my truck, beginning the hour-and-a-half trip to my mother's house. As Lucy processes the decedent into the coroner facility, I am moments away from telling my mother that her other daughter has died.

. . .

She weighs a hundred and ten pounds when the coroner examines her. She is five foot four and has long blond hair. She appears older than her twenty-four years. Her pupils are equal in diameter. There are noted needle marks and damaged veins consistent with IV drug use. She has tattoos on the left forearm, left bicep, right forearm, and the left lower quadrant of her abdomen. Her chest and breasts are unremarkable. Her nail beds are remarkable because of their bluish discoloration.

She is a young white female; cause of death is anoxia, cause of anoxia is pulmonary edema, cause of pulmonary edema is the toxic effects of methamphetamine. I know what these words mean now, know what happened in her body when meth flooded her system, how her lungs filled up with fluid, how she most likely hallucinated in her final moments before her brain shut down from lack of oxygen. Due to strong suspicion of drug overdose and evidence found at the scene, Lucy rules out an internal exam.

. . .

When I spoke on the phone to Lucy, days after Sarah's body was found, she told me that when she looked at my sister, she knew that she had been a good person who ended up in the wrong place. When she said she was sorry for my loss, I believe she meant it. I am okay with the last person to touch my sister's body being this woman, who took the time and care to talk to me. She explained to me the results of the toxicology report, and while I was surprised that Sarah died of a toxic meth overdose and not heroin, I did not fully take in what it all meant. This is why I ordered the coroner's report, expecting a few pages with numbers and exam results, Sarah's body reduced to data: 13.25 ml of heart blood is removed from Sarah's body and placed in two vials; 1 ml of vitreous humor is also taken.

When I read this, I somehow make the association between *humor* and *funny bone* and wonder why they took a sample from her elbow. In reality, vitreous humor is the transparent, jellylike tissue that sits behind the eye lens. Why did they need to pierce the most vulnerable places? I wish for her heart to be intact, even though I know it is eventually burned, turned to ash, and thrown into the sea. I resent these strangers pressing a needle into her eyes; Sarah didn't like anything touching them when she was alive.

The report details that three kinds of drugs are found in her system: benzodiazepine, methamphetamine, and opiates. The only drug found at a truly toxic level is meth. A chart shows the range for potentially effective levels of the drug (what would make you high) and the range for potentially toxic levels of the drug (what could kill you). The range for potentially toxic levels of meth is listed as 0.2 to 0.5 mg per liter of blood. Sarah's toxicology report shows a meth level of 2.7 mg per liter, more than ten times the lower end of the lethal range.

Many addicts live on the edge of overdose. If you had tested me at the height of my coke habit, I am sure my lab numbers would have been in the potentially toxic range. This is part of why addiction is dangerous: the more you use, the higher your tolerance gets, and you push at the line between high and dead. But the level of meth in Sarah's blood is not on the edge of overdose, it is miles past it.

The heart blood tells me everything and not nearly enough. It tells me that Sarah's death was inevitable, that it did not matter if Jack had found her four minutes or four days after shooting up; she was gone as soon as the milky white liquid entered her bloodstream. It tells me that either she had little experience shooting up meth or Ray knew exactly what he was doing when he slid the needle in. It tells me that her tired heart held on to whatever evidence it could until Lucy could look inside.

. . .

The coroner's report sits on my desk. Josh takes my hand, tries to pull me to a room where this narrative is not lying in wait. But I read it again and again, trying to understand the story. The ending is always the same: I am not there, Sarah is not laughing, and her feet, while still perched on the bathroom sink, are cold and dead.

My Heart

I sit down next to her. She doesn't see me. She is focused on her body's inability to live. She vomits into her open hands and puts her mouth to the wet warmth, trying to swallow it back into her body. She shits and tries to coax the waste back into her bowels. There is a mix of foam and blood coming out of her nose that she begs to return to her nostrils.

It's not working, I say. She looks at me, noticing my presence. She is more scared than I have ever seen her, more scared than the time she jumped in a wasp's nest and I had to pull her out, more scared than when she held our father's hand while he was dying.

I don't want to die, she says.

I know.

Can you help me?

I put my arm around her trembling body. She smells like sweet vinegar.

No, I say. *Why don't you tell me a story while we wait?*

She nods. She waits for a tremor to pass through her arms and legs before she starts.

I was going to have a baby. She pauses. *I thought that if I had a baby, I would never want to use again. I didn't know whose it was, but I didn't care. She was going to have eyes like ours and smell like warm milk and flour.*

What happened? I ask, gently, even though I already know.

I lost it, she says quietly. Her skin is tinged blue, and the whites of her eyes look like they can fall out of their sockets any second now. *She's here now, can you see her?*

I look around but only see Sarah.

No, I say.

She looks like us. She leans her head back against the bathroom door. *I fucked things up.*

We both did.

He killed me, you know?

I won't find that out for a while.

But one day?

Yes, I answer her, *one day. It won't do much good, but we will know.*

She looks relieved. *Good.* Her breathing is shallow and sporadic.

It won't be long now. I lean into her as I say this, hoping the warmth of my body will travel to her blood.

I'm scared. I think she is crying when she says this. I do not look at her. I lay her head in my lap and stroke her hair. Her body sings out with one final spasm. I hold tight until she is unbearably still.

Do you want to hear a story? I say. I know she will not respond.

I lay her on the tile floor. It is cold in here. She is cold. I lie next to her and wrap my arms around her body. I ignore the shit and vomit and mucus. The house is quiet save for the dog, who is knocking things over in the living room and howling at the bathroom door.

On the day you were born, you came out of the womb fighting, twisted your body in the birth canal but corrected your stuck shoulder before the doctor could go in himself. The first time I held you, I remember thinking you were tough.

This is where she began. I don't want her to forget.

We have time, I say. *Let me fill your bones with all the words I know.* On the first day, I speak of fairy queens and impossibly magic things. *You built altars deep in the forest, small kingdoms of wood, leaf, and flower. The structures remain, singing out the echoes of two girls who believed in everything.*

On the second day, I talk about the weight of trauma, the fragments of our lives we didn't author. *My divine love, don't forget our grandfather could breathe fire and our father spent his whole life looking for smoke. Did you know you were more than just his daughter? If she could, our mother would paint you back into existence. She would cover your body with gold leaf and feathers. She would crown you with deer horns and whisper witch words into your lungs until you took your second, first breath.*

On the third day, I tell her love is not enough. *I will search for you in every crowd. I will dream you are outside my door and only I can welcome you into my home. I am afraid you never felt welcome. You are welcome here. You are unequivocally welcome to take root inside my chest. Hollow out my rib cage, I will carry anything you want to leave there. If love were enough, you would still be here.*

On the evening of the fourth day, I hear the door of the house open and someone say, *What the fuck.*

I know I have to leave now.

I'm scared, I tell her. I consider shaking her. Footsteps come closer to the bathroom. *I'm scared,* I say again, loudly. But it is just me, and soon it will be just her and the boy who will find her body.

This is how she dies.

Hold Us

Josh and I are getting married. Amid the hue of grief, he is a warm, consistent light. He asks me to marry him long after we made the decision together, but we both wanted the moment of a ring and sweet words. He holds both of my hands and tells me that his world is larger than he thought possible because of our relationship. We eat sushi and watch his grandmother's diamond glint in the low-lit restaurant. We laugh at the stupid amount of love that is between us.

We plan our wedding during my last year of grad school. We book our venue for the July following my graduation. Josh is accepted into the same program I am finishing, so we figure that summer is the best time for both of us, before he starts school. We are getting married in Northern California, under a grove of eucalyptus trees overlooking the bay. We decide we will serve tacos from our favorite Mexican market. Josh brews all the beer for the reception, and my mother designs the beer labels for "Dukersen Ale," a joining of our last names. We ask our loved ones to make pies for dessert instead of ordering a cake. We decide that we don't want kids at the wedding. We tell everyone to bring their dogs, and I buy our dog, Charlotte, a flowered bow tie.

We ask Paul and Simon, a couple close to Sharon who I have known for over twenty years, to officiate our ceremony. I introduced Josh to them during a trip to New York, where they live and where I attended undergrad. We had dinner with them in their apartment near Harlem. It was one of those perfect meals where I can't remember anything we ate but can still recall the sound of Simon singing as he served dessert, the laughter as we listened to Paul tell a story, the night tipping toward the next day as we talked endlessly. When we left, I remember leaning against Josh's shoulder in the taxi and saying, "I want them to marry us."

A hundred friends and family sit on benches facing a wooden archway that our kind neighbor built for us. Tess has strung garlands of marigolds together and draped them over the redwood arch. My mother has laid down an aisle of brightly colored antique rugs from her home. Our reception site waits for us, a short walk away. It is a remodeled single-engine airplane hangar with high ceilings and a long, gleaming bar that was rescued from the local firehouse when it was torn down. Farm tables are lined with runners made of pages from our favorite books and hold mason jars filled with local flowers, lovingly arranged by our friends.

I do feel the weight of Sarah as I hold my bouquet to my chest. The flowers are both petals and ash, leaves and bone. She is both here and so very not here. I experience a version of déjà vu all day; she glimmers at the edge of every moment. I joke with Tess, who is one of my brides-maids, that if Sarah were here, she would probably hit on one of the groomsmen or cry so loudly during the vows that everyone would pay attention to her. We laugh. We'd both do anything to have her here with us.

Josh and I listen to Paul start speaking while we wait for our entrance. "Couples don't live in isolation, but in communities," he says. "We, their community, create the environment that gives shape to their relationship, and so how we hold them is a responsibility and a great gift to them." He goes on, but my heart has already tipped over, and I am full of love not just for Josh but for the group of people waiting for us, who have held us for so long.

The ceremony is magical and cold and perfect. The fog rolls in, and I can't feel my hands. Paul and Simon sing a duet from *La Cage aux Folles*, and everyone is laughing. I say my vows first.

I say, "I have never been more certain of anything than I have been of loving you."

I say, "My world is infinitely larger and more beautiful and I am acutely aware of the joy and magic you bring into my life every day."

I say, "I will hold on to the truth of this moment— which is that in a world that can be hard and sad, we are lucky enough to stand among those we love and share the brilliance of our commitment."

I say, "You dazzle me, my love. You have brought a lightness into my life that I didn't think was possible, and I commit to creating a life with you that is rooted in that radiance."

I say a great many things that fill the space between us. There is only one moment when it feels like my chest will crack and I won't be able to continue. Josh looks at me intently when my voice shakes at "a world that can be hard and sad," and the true meaning sings in a language that only we can speak: *This is a world where my beautiful, infuriating little sister is dead, but you, Josh Duke, have wrapped my grief in something I can only call holy because this is as close to understanding the cosmos as I will ever get.*

Josh speaks. He says, "In all the chaos and uncertainty this universe can afford to us, I am calm and centered and loved and loving within your embrace."

He says, "With you, the world is in focus. Everything makes sense. I don't need to apologize for being myself. The world, my world, our world, is bigger with us in each other's lives. Together, we do the things we couldn't do alone."

He says, "You, we, are something special and cosmic and full of colors not found anywhere else, constantly painting a picture of love and devotion and adventure and companionship that when I reach the end of my long life and look back at that picture, I can say, 'That was a life well-lived, with the best person I could live it with.'"

He says, "I will plant succulents on our patio because I will be too busy having fun with you to remember to water anything regularly. I will kiss your eyes good night before we sleep and wake up every morning smelling the back of your neck."

He says, "You have my heart, and I have yours. It's buried in my chest. It will always be there, beating forever to remind me of all the things I've promised."

We leave in a flurry of red, pink, and white petals. For a moment, Sarah is standing next to me, grinning and arms outstretched. I can almost remember what she smells like. In the blur of cheers and flowers and love, she is gone, and I am left with my shining partner, walking toward my second life.

Knowing

I will never know exactly how she died. I can write her death a thousand times and still come no closer to understanding what happened on November 19, 2013. I can only write around the edges of her ghost.

· · ·

I know she died. That is the truth of the thing that shudders inside my body. This desire to investigate is an attempt to distract from that knowing.

· · ·

Grief does not leave our bodies. Oh, if I could open up my chest, I would take you to the dark space inside my second heart. Do you see her? She is cowering in the corner, guarded by other monsters I cannot yet face.

· · ·

We grow around the hurt, it is not displaced. The unbearable pain is compacted but retains its weight.

I have a good life. There are joy and dogs and perfectly made cups of coffee. I watch bad movies with my closest friend and eat popcorn in the dark. I sing off-key and do a little dance when Josh makes banana pancakes. Charlotte snores at our feet and tries to kiss my face when I give her a treat. These are things that have surrounded that dark, tender spot I am still afraid to touch.

. . .

I wake up in the middle of the night and have to check if Josh is still breathing. I place my shaking hand on his chest and wait for an exhalation.

. . .

I will never be a light thing. This is what I know.

ACKNOWLEDGMENTS

Thank you to my agent, Matt McGowan, for taking a chance on this strange, sad book and reminding me that this is only just the beginning.

Many thanks to my editor, Callie Garnett, who understood the heart of this story from our first phone call to the last changed word. I will never look at these pages without hearing your voice as we read through each and every sentence over the phone. Thank you, for your attention to detail, for your genuine love of language and sentence structure, for believing in this work even on the days I did not.

My experience with Bloomsbury has been incredible—the sheer amount of enthusiasm and excitement has made my writer heart feel so full. Thank you to every single person who has had a hand in this process. Cindy Loh and Nancy Miller for leading this amazing team. The marketing and publicity departments for their tireless work. I am so grateful for Marie Coolman, Valentina Rice, and Laura Keefe. Special thanks to Tara Kennedy, publicist extraordinaire, Nicole Jarvis, marketing maven, and Akshaya Iyer, production pro.

Thank you to Myunghee Kwon, who designed a cover that was more than anything I could have dreamed of.

This book would not have been possible without the guidance and support of the CalArts MFA program. Janet Sarbanes, for showing me the joys of fiction and reading with such care. Doug Kearney, for providing a space for me to write terrible poetry and teaching me how to bring a sense of immediacy to my nonfiction. Tisa Bryant, for her incredible reading lists and generous feedback. Matias Viegener, who showed me the value of bringing tenderness into a classroom. Mike Byrant, my pedagogical friend, I learn so much from our continued conversations.

To Marjorie Spain, whose open heart even in the midst of grief served as the kindest touchstone during this process. To Alecia Workman-Manzano for showing me the power of saying no (and the power of really good shoes).

Special thanks to my mentor, Brian Evenson, for the Facebook posts about pet lemon trees, the endless encouragement to get my work into the world, and the most challenging and exacting feedback a writer can get—"Best?"

I want to extend my gratitude to Nelly Reifler, Penny Wolfson, Doug MacHugh, and Fanchon Scheier; you've all had a hand in shaping how I create art—thank you.

Special thanks to my mentor (and one of my favorite writers), Mary Morris, who has been telling me since I was nineteen that I was meant to be a writer. I finally listened! You taught me how to craft a perfect sentence and the importance of a daily writing practice. You have been a constant in my adult life and I am so grateful to know you.

Thank you to my fellow writers, for reading and listening and holding me through this process. My Future Ghosts, Char Simpson and Sara Selevitch. Ian Kappos for copyediting an early draft. Erin Khar, for writing the book I wish had existed long ago. Janet Albaugh for your humor and tenacity. Maggie Lange for being my pitching partner and novel buddy.

Special thanks to Rosa Boshier, whose work inspires me, whose friendship has kept me sane, whose intelligence and humor dazzle me.

Endless gratitude to Emily Maloney: I don't know if I could have gotten through this process without you. Thank you for listening to all my potato feelings, providing pictures of good boi horses, and telling me exactly how to get my shit together.

Thank you to my dear friends—Ally, Suzanne, Kathryn, Mara, Zoe, Anne, Andrea, Lisa Hedgie Enge—the chicken whisperer, Rob Enge, Jenny Finch, Beth Rowe, Brandy Trigueros, Kaili Walker, Leslie Legg, Paul Browde, Simon Fortin, Kim Searcy, John Grau, Darlyn Smith, Debbie O'Brien and Debbie Vosevich.

To Tess and Ilena for loving Sarah for exactly who she was.

Thank you to Jed, without whom school would not have been possible. To Sharon, for your magical house in the woods, for always swimming with us, for showing me the joys of sobriety. To my mom, for filling my life with animals, beautiful art, books, and elven lineage.

To my spouse and dearest friend, Josh—quite simply, you are the best around. You live in every page of this story because your love and puns and coffee held me throughout. Thank you for surrounding this dark with the most radiant light.

And finally, always, my love and gratitude to Sarah for being wild and strong and wily. I would erase every page if it meant having you back.

A NOTE ON THE AUTHOR

Rose Andersen received her MFA in writing from the California Institute of the Arts, where she was awarded the Emi Kuriyama Thesis Prize. Her essays have appeared in *The Cut*, *Glamour*, and other publications. She lives in LA with her spouse, Josh, and their dog, Charlotte.
@roseandersen
roseandersenwrites.com